THE POWER OF RHYTHM

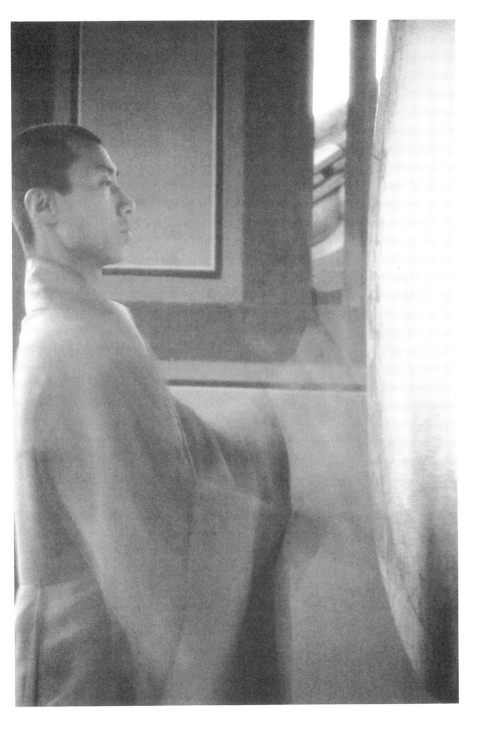

Acknowledgements:

Gay Gaer Luce for permission to quote from BODY TIME,
Pantheon Book, 1971.

TAO TE CHING by Lao Tsu, translated by Gia-fu Feng
and Jane English. Copyright © 1972 by Gia-fu Feng
and Jane English. Reprinted by permission of Alfred A. Knopf Inc.

Logo: Ernst Graf
Translator: Tim Nevill
Editor: Peter Greenwood
Technical Illustration: Rennie Innis
Photographs: Reinhard Flatischler and Heidrun Hoffman

"I offer my deep love and gratitude to my wife Cornelia, who supported me with her feminine wisdom as I wrote this book."

Reinhard Flatischler

In the deepest layers of consciousness, every human being lives in perfect harmony with rhythm. For many of us, awareness of our natural connection with rhythm has disappeared. By re-establishing a connection with the Power of Rhythm, TaKeTiNa reveals new qualities of life, thus enhancing human development.

Knowing that rhythm consciousness connects us with our inner-selves and leads us back to the wisdom of sharing our common humanity, I dedicate this book to all drummers of the world. May their powerful pulsations help heal our planet so that one day all races may play together in perfect synchronisation.

TABLE OF CONTENTS

4 (Continued)

5 ARCHETYPES OF RHYTHM

6 THE HUMAN BODY AS MUSICAL INSTRUMENT

7 CREATING WITH THE ELEMENTS OF RHYTHM

Note: The large numbers appearing in the margins of the text refer to the recorded musical examples on the CD, included in this book.

RECORDING MUSICAL EXAMPLES   Page

INTRODUCTION

The Drum – it's one of my creative addictions. I love to play it, listen to it, talk about it.

I've developed a voracious appetite for its variations and rhythms. Recently, at a TaKeTiNa workshop with Reinhard Flatischler, a master percussionist and composer born in Austria, and his partner and wife Cornelia Flatischler, I experienced a deep healing through the vibrations and rhythms of the drum.

As I walked into the workshop I was surprised to learn that rather than playing drums, we were to use our bodies as our instruments. I also discovered that some of the workshop participants were accomplished musicians and percussionists while some of us, like myself, were total beginners. The rest of us covered every level in-between.

We launched right in with the instructions to step from side to side with our feet in a one-two rhythm. Soon after establishing this basic beat we were asked to clap our hands in a second rhythm, followed shortly by joining our voices in a third rhythm. So, we are simultaneously stepping a rhythm, clapping a second one, and vocalizing a third one. Each session of this physical exploration of the layering of rhythms, one on top of the other, lasts for no shorter than an hour and sometimes longer. This gives us time to sink into the groove. Unlike other drum classes, where we are counting rhythms in a linear fashion, this was an extraordinary, non-linear way of learning. My thinking mind is by-passed and the information goes directly into my body. In fact, my thinking mind just hinders the entire process. I couldn't be thinking the rhythms to happen, I could only feel them into being.

I was successful beyond my wildest imaginings. I know that, had I stumbled into this class as all these people were singing, clapping, and stamping, I would have thought I was in the wrong workshop. I would have assumed these were master percussionists and would have gone searching for the beginners class.

But here we were, maybe 25 of us, all swaying, and clapping, and singing intricate patterns that connect us in a single, rhythmic community. Occasionally, and even often, each of us falls out of the rhythm and that is part of the teaching: by falling out, we can experience falling in. There are no mistakes, just humor at falling out and falling in.

During all this, Cornelia stands in the middle of the circle softly stamping her feet. Her ankles are adorned with several rows of Indian bells. At the same time, she is playing a bass beat on a large Brazilian surdo that she has strapped to her shoulders for comfort. This deep sounding drum provides an unvarying pulsation. Simultaneously, Reinhard is guiding us in rhythmic chants as he makes rounds inside the circle while playing a counter point to the rhythms on a Brazilian berimbao.

I can feel my excitement as he comes close to me. I want to show-off my skill, I'm actually doing it. And, as he comes closer my mind takes over, I lose the beat. He is in front of me and we laugh as I go back go back to the basic step with Cornelia's drum.

At some point, Cornelia starts to fade the rhythm, not changing it in any way, but making it softer and softer. Gradually we abandon our stepping, chanting and clapping, and lie down on the floor, feeling the relaxed way it holds us up. The beat becomes barely audible and then fades from the ears altogether.

Suddenly, I feel the beat continuing to play in my body. No longer can I hear it with my outside ears, but, by switching to inside ears, I hear the rhythm pulsing boldly in my body. My entire being is filled with rhythm. I'm fascinated by this vibration and begin to suspect it has always lived inside me; I just didn't have ears to hear it before now.

I'm feeling a deep, deep peace. Not only has my mental chatter calmed down but the very cells of my body are relaxed. Feelings of great contentment sweep over me and I'm safe in the universe. In this moment of quiet calm, I have a flash of insight about my own birth.

Some time ago, I heard a tape of the sound environment of a fetus in this mother's womb. Surprisingly, this is not the quiet calm one normally associates with the womb. It is a loud environment filled with the pulsating rhythms of her heartbeat and blood flow. There is a counterpoint to this rhythm when she speaks and laughs.

Like many others who were born in the early forties, I was taken away from my mother right after birth and put in a hospital nursery with lots of bright lights, strange sounds, and crying babies. Suddenly, I was in an environment devoid of my mother's rhythmic heartbeat.

All this memory is flooding back to me as I lie on the floor feeling peaceful and calm, hearing the cosmic rhythm playing my body as if I am a drum. As I'm listening with my inside ears, a deep healing is taking place. The fright of that first moment of mother and child separation is healed as I feel the pulsation inside me. No longer searching outside myself for the safe and assuring rhythms of life, I now know they are within me and always have been.

I'm deeply grateful to Cornelia and Reinhard Flatischler for their undying dedication and for my own personal growth through their TaKeTiNa rhythm process. Even if you've never touched a drum, I encourage you to experience this process, it will be life-changing, I guarantee it.

Justine Willis Toms
Co-founder and Managing Producer of *New Dimensions Radio*
Author of *Small Pleasures: Finding Grace in a Chaotic World*

1

AN INVITATION

I began my journey into rhythm by studying with the master drummers of Asia, Africa and Latin America. Their drums seemed like pieces of an unknown mosaic—an image that eluded me. Each drum unfolded the fascination of its own rhythmic world, but no matter how hard I tried, I couldn't discover a connection between those drums and my everyday life in Europe. One day, I came across a story by Gustav Meyrink entitled "The Buddha Is My Refuge." It told of a musician, a cellist, whose sole wish was to travel to India so that he might absorb the teachings of Gautama Buddha. But he was poor and lived all alone in a ramshackle hut. On holy days, he took out a sheet of glass, fixed it to his table and scattered grains of sand onto the glass. As he drew his bow across the edge of the glass, the sand danced and formed delicate star shapes; this was his only pleasure.

For many years, he quietly played his cello in the local taverns and gradually saved enough money for his journey, although by now he had become white-haired and frail. As he sat looking at the money lying on the table, he suddenly forgot what he had been working toward for so many years. There came a knock at the door and the violinist with whom he often played entered. "We're collecting for the children of the poor today," said the fiddler softly. The old man gave all the money on the table to him. When his friend left, the old man, as so often on holy days, fixed the sheet of glass to the table and spread out the fine grains of sand. He drew his bow across the edge of the glass and once again the sand danced into delicate star shapes.

And as these stars and forms came into being, changing and disappearing, the musician thought gloomily of the Buddha's teachings about suffering: its birth, its dispersal and the way leading to its eradication. It then happened that through one of the holes in the roof a snowflake fell on the table—a tiny, delicate, symmetrical star. It remained for a moment and disappeared. Suddenly, like lightning rending the darkness, the old man's heart was filled with the light of understanding. He realized that the star shape of the snowflake was the same as the stars formed by the vibrating sand. Now he understood that everything in the temporal world, all forms and beings, have their origin in pulsations; imperceptible and inaudible pulsations concealed within the cosmos.

And so, through this story, I gained a glimmer of hope that a common ground exists beneath the many kinds of music I knew; that *rhythm* is a power which unites all living things.

Years later, when I was giving a concert with Korean musicians in Seoul, a man who emanated great openness came to me during the intermission; it was pleasant to feel his tranquility as he looked at me. Finally he spoke: "I could sense what you're trying to express through your playing, but I think that something inside of you says NO." He smiled as he left.

Although his words confused and upset me, they spoke to something deep within me; they re-awoke the feeling that something remained outwardly unexpressed in my playing. It was clear to me that I had to meet this man again, that I wanted to play for him and learn from him. The Korean musicians with whom I had given this concert explained to me that I had just met Kim Sok Chul, one of the few surviving Korean shamans. Later they told me a great deal about the music of these Korean shamans: that it was several thousand years old, was from the *Tunguse* people and that nobody had any precise information about it. They also said that in all of Korea only a few shamans still employed the ancient knowledge of healing rhythms and music. Many months, even years, would pass before an outsider would gain access to their ceremonies and music. A year later I was invited by the director of the Goethe Institute in Seoul to visit Korea to gather information on shaman rhythms. I felt this was a clear sign for me so I dropped everything and set off for Korea.

On my very first day there, I met Kim Sok Chul again and he invited me to stay with him. My discovery of Korean rhythms thus began in a totally unexpected way; instead of recording the various rhythms in order to analyze them at leisure in Europe, I sat daily for many hours at the *tschanggo*, the most important shaman drum of Korea. As I learned the first sequence of beats, Kim Sok Chul brought me time and again to a point which made me feel that something within me was not entirely involved. I encountered very clearly someone within myself who said NO: someone I had never known before. But now as Kim Sok Chul sat alongside me and played his drum, I clearly sensed how freely his rhythms unfolded onto a much higher plane than mine. His strange smile seemed to come from that plane and it expressed a profound oneness with his being. I gradually despaired of ever contacting my inner obstruction. I could feel it but it remained inexplicable. Playing was a great joy for me and I had a deep respect for the power of the rhythms I experienced when Kim Sok Chul took me to the ceremonies. He didn't seem bothered about my increasing unrest and calmly showed me one rhythm after another. But, with a smile, he would always dismiss my questions about the effects of those rhythms.

Kim Sok Chul had planned a journey for us to attend various ceremonies but just before we were to leave, I suddenly came down with a high fever, forcing me to cancel both the trip and my drum practice. The doctor's diagnosis was dysentery, and although he started intensive treatment immediately, my health worsened by the day. I thought about flying back to Europe but even that was too much for me in my weakened state. When Kim Sok Chul returned from his journey, he immediately visited me and announced that he had prepared a healing ceremony and would come for me on the following day. He left before I could object.

I felt paralyzed, depleted and all of my limbs were in pain. In this state how would I be able to stand the loud music which I had so often experienced? How could Korean rhythms improve my condition when even the strongest medicines had failed? Suddenly these shaman ceremonies seemed like nothing more than superstition and I realized I had lost faith in the effect of such rhythms. I was very afraid. When Kim Sok Chul and his friends came the next day to pick me up, I was determined not to proceed with the ceremony. He sensed my resistance even though I was unable to express it. He stood next to me for a long time and although he did not say a word, he emanated something that allowed me to trust him. I agreed to go.

But when we arrived at the site of the ceremony, I was terrified again. Kim Sok Chul had vanished and I felt alone in a world of dark powers. My pain increased and it all seemed like an endless nightmare. The music began thunderously; the shrill sounds of the instruments splintered my thoughts and I fell into a state in which thinking was impossible. I recognized my surroundings and yet I found myself in a completely different world—a world full of feelings that I had never experienced before. I felt parts of my body disassemble and then re-connect; I saw my body assume various colors, each of which produced a certain indescribable bodily sensation within and I sank ever deeper into a state of which I have no recollection.

When I regained consciousness, the sun was shining into the little room in Kim Sok Chul's house where I was lying. I was very tired but feeling better. Soon I fell into a long, deep sleep. In the following weeks I began to recover and I gradually saw that at the decisive moment I was unable to believe in what I had long sought—*the power of rhythm*. The NO within me finally became apparent. It was a NO toward life that had built up during my childhood and it lived in a totally unconscious. part of me. This NO, which was a source of constant fear, doubt and weakness, surfaced in my apprenticeship with Kim Sok Chul and began to melt away during the ceremony.

And so there arose in me the knowledge that rhythm can reach deep levels of my consciousness and that to connect with the power of rhythm means to expand awareness. I discovered that rhythm as a path does not depend on intellectual achievement or ability and is open to both men and women as equals. It leads toward a oneness of musical and human consciousness and guides us directly to the underlying power of all life. Rhythm touches deep chords of resonance in our ancestral memories; whenever we connect with other human beings through rhythmic music, dance, or drumming, the memory of humankind as one family arises. Although we remain individuals, it is easy to remember our common humanity—a deeply healing knowledge, especially in today's world. I invite you to let this book guide you on your own path of rhythm.

Creating your own vision of rhythm by understanding the effects of various rhythmic phenomena is one way of understanding. *Experiencing* rhythm is the other. You will find both approaches in this book— chapters that invite you to reflect on rhythmic phenomena and also many practical exercises which will enable you to experience rhythm *in* your body and to play rhythms *with* your body. If you attempt to learn these exercises as quickly as possible you will miss the point, so please take plenty of time with each step and remember to enjoy your body during the exercise so that you may *feel* how your body reacts to various rhythmic phenomena. In this way, rhythm will become a conscious part of your life.

As I made my way through the rhythms of various world cultures, I found in all of them the same rhythmic archetypes underlying different forms of music. From these rhythmic archetypes I developed a rhythmic bodywork, the beginning level of which is herein presented. In this work, vocal rhythms, clapping and elementary steps affect one another in a great variety of ways. The rhythmic voice plays a central role. Your body is the only instrument you need to play in these exercises and you may then transfer this experience to any musical instrument.

Drum languages are found in all cultures. And in addition, there are rhythm words and syllables which have had a parallel development. TA KI,

GA MA LA and TA KE TI NA are mantras that are frequently used in my rhythmic bodywork. They have no meaning, but their constant repetition while connecting them with different movements, allows them to go deeply into our consciousness, arousing our own ancient knowledge of rhythm. When I did my first workshops twenty-two years ago, many participants would ask me "When will we do TA KE TI NA again?" And so the path to rhythm, which gradually emerged out of my own development, called itself "TA KE TI NA."

In this book, you will encounter terms unlike those you may already know. *Meter, bar line* and *syncopation* may be valid concepts in Western music but the bar line concept doesn't fit Indian or various kinds of African music. All terms used in this book do have their counterparts in standard Western terminology, but they also apply to the music of other cultures as well. My aim is to make those terms clear through a bodily experience. You will meet various rhythmic terms time and again and get to know them from different perspectives. In this way, they will become familiar and eventually clear and straight forward.

In classical tradition, we first comprehend the structures intellectually and then transfer that to the body and the playing. In non-European cultures, however, the bodily experience comes first so that with subsequent reflection the rhythmic structure, already understood by the body, becomes clear. Both ways can be used to advantage if we develop their possibilities and incorporate them in the exercises so that they complement each other. Please join me now as we take our first step onto the path of rhythm.

2

THE RHYTHMIC BODY

This chapter will guide you through a variety of practical and elementary rhythmic exercises which require no prior experience. It is, however, essential that you take your time with these exercises and do them in a place where you won't be disturbed. You may have someone read the instructions to you but make sure your reader's pace is comfortable for you. Or you might try recording the instructions yourself and thereby discover how well you know your own pace. All the rhythmic phenomena you encounter in these exercises will be encountered again and again throughout this book—each time in a new light but with a familiar feeling.

Experiencing Inner Pulsation

You can either sit or lie on your back for this first experience of rhythm. Choose a position that allows you to relax in the present moment and is conducive to "inner listening." If thoughts occur, let them drift away, like clouds in the sky, and direct your attention to the sensing of your body. When you feel ready, place your hand where the pulse can easily be felt such as in the neck, wrist, or abdomen. Take time to establish contact with your pulse and *listen* to it with your finger tips. First feel the pulse itself, and then gradually direct your attention to the interval between each beating pulse.

As soon as you can feel your pulse clearly, gradually reduce contact between your finger tips and the pulse. When you reach the point where you just barely feel the pulse, stay at this threshold between barely feeling and not feeling. Allow yourself time to feel if the pulsation seems to spread from the point of contact to other parts of the body. It may then be that you gradually feel your pulse elsewhere in the body. Finally, remove your hand from the point of contact with the pulse and be aware of your *entire* body. Allow the rhythmic experience to linger within yourself until you feel ready to stop.

Experiencing the "Inner Voice"

This exercise can also be done either lying down or sitting. As soon as you've found a position that feels right, close your eyes and direct attention toward the boundary between your body and the surrounding space. You can perceive that frontier by viewing your body from within—and also by sensing the boundaries between different parts of the body and the surrounding area. Now let the sounds of different syllables arise within you and allow them to form a repeating sequence. If you whisper this sequence over and over, a rhythmic flow of various sounds begins. Feel your lips move while whispering and how the rhythmic flow of your voice streams out of your mouth. Your voice can expand into the room through your bodily boundaries. Now let your voice become louder and louder and listen to it gradually fill the space around you. Allow time to sense the movement of your lips, tongue, mouth, and vocal chords. Put your hands on your throat and chest so you can feel the vibration of your voice.

When you feel the rhythmic flow of the voice *in your body*, allow your voice to grow quieter. Pay attention to the way the movements of your mouth change as you gradually return to whispering. Now let the whispering become ever quieter. At some point, your voice will become inaudible but keep moving your lips even though the rhythmic flow of your words is drawn inward. While you continue to do so ask yourself: "Am I speaking now or am I listening?" It could happen that you experience how speaking and listening become one in this process. Listen to how and where your voice continues to sound within you; it may be that you still clearly feel its movement. By reducing your lip movements, can you make your inner voice become quieter until it finally yields to an inner silence? Allow that rhythmic experience to linger until the experience feels complete.

The Interaction of Pulse and Voice

Once again, you can either sit or lie down for this rhythmic experience. As with all the exercises, first try to relax. Enjoy the tranquility for a while and then see if you can feel your pulse somewhere in the body without actually touching it. Next put your hand where the pulse is to be felt and take time to contact your inner pulsation. As you feel your pulse, allow a sound to arise within yourself which imitates the sound of your pulse. First try to find this sound with your inner voice and when you have found it, link it with the pulse. The pulsating of your heart will thus gradually be made audible. Take time to feel the pulse and voice unite and observe how your pulse reacts as it connects with your voice. Does it become stronger or weaker, faster or slower, or does it remain the same?

Gradually separate your voice from the pulse and return to listening. Now direct your attention to the interval between the pulse beats. When you feel ready give an inner voice to the syllable "GO" at the mid-point of each one of these intervals. If you find it difficult at the beginning then pause before you continue whispering GO. The succession of pulse and voice thus becomes:

| Heartbeat | ♡ | ♡ | ♡ | ♡ | ♡ | ♡ | ♡ | ♡ |
| Voice | GO | GO | GO | GO | GO | GO | GO | GO |

Don't worry if your pulse becomes difficult to feel or, even, at times, irregular—this is a normal occurrence. Once again pay attention to how your pulse reacts. Does it become stronger or weaker, faster or slower? How loud can the GO become before you are no longer able to sense the pulse? Allow your voice to become quieter again and return to whispering GO and finally to speaking with your inner voice. Perhaps the interval in your pulse can now be felt very clearly. When you have returned to quietness end the exercise at your leisure.

The Flow of the Breath

This time, lie on your back on the floor, pulling your heels toward your buttocks so that your knees bend and the soles of your

on the floor. Allow yourself to feel how gravity affects
-you can allow yourself to be supported by the floor.
lly direct attention to your nose. Feel how air streams
tnrough it into your body—and how it flows out again. Follow this
in and out flow attentively. When the air flows through the nose into
your body, give it space and allow it to fill you. When you sense
that the movement is reversed and the air flows out, then feel how
you let it go. Keep your attention on this process of releasing until
you reach that point where the flowing ceases and a moment of stillness occurs before the air once again enters your body. You can
experience that moment as one of *letting be*. Remain attentive to the
flowing of your breath, enjoying how the *releasing*, the *letting be*,
and the *allowing to enter* always follow one another of their own
accord: The *releasing* when exhaling, the *letting be* at the moment
of transition and the *allowing to enter* while inhaling.

When you feel the moment has come for ending the exercise,
allow yourself to feel whether more air is flowing through the right
or the left nostril. As soon as you feel that, turn onto your side so
that the freer nostril is above the other. In that position follow the
breath for a while and let the exercise gradually conclude.

The Encounter of Breath and Pulse

Assume the same position in which you experienced the flowing of the breath. Once again, feel how the soles of your feet contact the floor. Allow yourself time to experience the rhythmic flow
of your breathing and place your hand where you can feel your pulse.
Here you make contact with a second rhythmic movement within
yourself. At times your breathing may be more evident than your
pulse and vice versa, but there may also be moments when both
rhythms feel equally clear. Notice during those moments how the
two rhythms are different but nevertheless related.

Now direct more attention to sensing the pulse, linking it with
the syllables GA MA LA. Speak the syllables with your *inner voice*
so that each pulse-beat is accompanied by one syllable. When you
sense that the pulse and the inner voice come together effortlessly
try to extend your inhaling *(allowing to enter)* through one recitation of GA MA LA. The exhaling *(releasing)* and the pause *(letting
be)* then both stretch over two recitations of GA MA LA. See if you
can feel the flowing of your breath encounter the pulsating of your
heart during this process. At first, this link may seem impossible.

If you lose the sense of your pulse, it may be a sign that your body is not presently ready for such an encounter. I ask you to respect that sign from your body.

If you feel that the pulse and breathing link up effortlessly, stay with that for as long as you enjoy it. If you want to lengthen your breathing cycle then your inner voice could replace GA MA LA with MU SAN GA LA. As before each pulse-beat is accompanied by one syllable. Inhalation now occurs during *one* recitation of MU SAN GA LA and exhalation and letting be occurs during *two* recitations of MU SAN GA LA.

Connecting Breath, Voice, and Walking: The Flowing Walk

Begin by standing with eyes closed, and take time to sense the soles of your feet making contact with the floor and gradually direct attention to the breath. Remember the feeling of *letting in*, *letting be* and *letting out* and notice how your breathing occurs of its own accord.

Once you begin enjoying the flow of your breath, gradually transfer your body weight to one side. Observe whether the flow of your breathing changes once the weight has been completely transferred to one side and the other leg is lifted. If you feel insecure, open your eyes for a moment. Feel the inflowing and outflowing of the breath a few times in this position. At the start of an exhalation return the raised leg to the floor. Make contact first with the heel, allowing your step to be just as flowing and tranquil as is your breathing. Slowly transfer body weight to the other side so that this movement occurs with the release of breath. As the next breath-wave flows in you may sense the other leg lifting itself. Let the foot touch the ground with the beginning of the next exhalation and observe that a flowing quality becomes increasingly apparent in your walking.

Allow the movement of your slow walking to be guided by the movement of your breath. If you like, gradually begin to accompany each release of breath with a humming sound. Maybe you will sense a connection between the sound of your voice and the contact with the floor established by your steps—a new step for every release of the breath. You will thus enter a *flowing walk* at one with the rhythm of your breath. Stay with that for as long as you enjoy it and end the exercise by releasing the connection between your walking and breathing.

Connecting Pulse, Voice, and Walking: The Pulsating Walk

The pulse is your central rhythmic power. With it, you directly encounter your own being. So take a little more time than usual for this exercise and pay attention to internal signals. If you notice that the exercise is becoming too much of a strain, feel free to stop at any time. It may be that the pulse is at one moment clear and at another less so. That is a sign of its vitality. If you can't feel your pulse please pay attention to that sign of your inner rhythm and assume that your pulse is not ready for such an encounter at present.

Start the exercise in a standing position and once again feel the soles of your feet contacting the floor. Then place a hand on your pulse. Give yourself time to feel whether you want the hand to be on your neck, wrist or abdomen. By whispering a sound, allow every pulse you feel to become audible—as you have before. The longer you let this pulsation affect you, the more intensely it will be felt. If you clearly feel the pulsing of your heart, try to take a step together with any single pulse of your heartbeat. Make this movement as small as possible and see if your pulse reacts to the encounter with your step. When you feel ready take another step in conjunction with a single pulse and sense the simultaneity of inner and outer movement. As your pulse allows you, gradually start walking in time with it, taking a step on every second, third or fourth pulse-beat. You will thus begin a pulsating-walk which is directly linked to your inner rhythm. Continue walking for as long as you enjoy it. Release contact with the pulse, lie down and allow yourself time to sense this rhythmic experience as it lingers within you.

The Interaction of Clapping and Voice

Before I guide you into the next experience, I want to briefly explain a few symbols found throughout this book. The symbols are part of a system known as "pulsation notation." Standard Western notation shows the *duration* of sounds, whereas this "pulsation notation" shows what *happens* on each pulse and with which movement of the body.

○	=	Clap
TA, KI, GO	=	Voice Syllables
ᗡ or —	=	Step
•	=	Empty Pulse
o	=	Pulse

The following exercise can be done either sitting or standing—whichever is more comfortable. Again place a hand in contact with your pulse and link your heart-beat with your voice by saying the syllable GO on each pulse-beat. As you let your voice become louder and louder, remove the hand. The pulse now sounds out with your voice:

Heartbeat	♡	♡	♡	♡	♡	♡	♡	♡
Voice	GO	GO	GO	GO	GO	GO	GO	GO

If you can feel the pulse clearly, turn your attention to the mid-point of the interval between the syllables. When you can hear that mid-point, try to mark it with a soft clap.

Clap	○	○	○	○	○	○	○	○
Voice	GO	GO	GO	GO	GO	GO	GO	GO

If it is too difficult to hear the mid-point of the interval, take your time and allow the pulsation of your voice to become a little slower. If you have no trouble clapping precisely between the pulses of your voice, then let that pulsation gradually get faster. To start with, increase the tempo minimally and observe your body's reaction. Increase the tempo gradually to the point where it becomes impossible for you to clap at the mid-point of the interval. Keep sensing the bodily changes and notice how different you feel as the clapping and voice finally coincide when you have reached your limit. Pause at this point and take time to sense what your breathing, your arm muscles and your shoulders tell you at this moment. Let the exercise slowly end itself.

Stepping at the Mid-Point of the Interval

Stand quietly in a relaxed manner and again direct attention to the contact your feet make with the floor. When you feel at ease, start clapping again at about the same speed as your pulse. Make sure that the single claps are resonant but quiet and all at about the same volume level. Now add your voice to this rhythmic process by speaking the syllable GO with each clap. The clapping and the voice thus pulsate together.

Make sure that your tempo remains the same and once again direct attention to the interval. When you sense the mid-point of the interval try to step exactly at that point.

Give yourself sufficient time and try to discern where the impulse for these steps arises in your body. If you have difficulty achieving a slow walk, then take a step only after every second or third clap and also slow down the tempo. If you succeed in stepping at the mid-point of each interval, take time to register the accompanying feeling in your body. Remember that the basic pulsation is derived from the voice and the clapping. Sense this relationship between voice, clapping and steps for as long as you find it enjoyable, and then return to a standing position. Let the voice and clapping become ever quieter and end the exercise at your leisure.

Various Interactions Between Voice, Clapping, and Steps

You can try this last exercise while you're taking a walk. Choose a path that allows a tranquil, pulsating gait. Listen to the steps you take and also try to perceive the interval between the steps. When you sense the mid-point in those intervals, make it audible by clapping softly.

Again, pay attention to the bodily feeling linked with the walking. When you feel ready, add your voice as a third element. When your right foot touches the ground speak the syllable TA and when the left foot touches, say KI. Your voice and these steps pulsate together while the clapping occurs at the mid-point of the interval. Let this relationship between voice, clapping, and steps affect you for awhile and feel how the sound of your voice is linked to your steps.

Observe what happens when you change your voice accompaniment from the steps to your clapping. Say the syllable GO with every clap but keep walking at the same pulsation. Allow sufficient time for this new relationship of voice, clapping, and steps to take effect. If this is easy, then alternate your voice between the steps and the clapping several times. Accompany the clapping with the syllable GO and your steps with TA and KI in succession. Play with that for as long as you enjoy it and then return to normal walking.

As you continue your stroll, sense this rhythmic experience lingering within you—an awakening of the power of rhythm that lies deep within each and every body.

3

PULSATION

Having experienced the great variety of rhythms within the body and how our consciousness reacts to them we may now ask: What is the relationship of body rhythms and musical rhythms and how does the enormous variety of musical rhythms develop out of primary rhythmic elements? We begin with the most fundamental relationship: *pulse* and *interval.*

Pulse and Interval

You have felt your heartbeat—do you remember the interval *between* those pulses? With every step you sensed your foot contacting the floor—do you remember the interval *between* the steps? The interval exists between one foot striking the ground and the next. If you *live through* this period of time by directing your attention to this interval as you walk you will have a different experience of walking than you do when concentrating only on the feet striking the ground.

Pulse and interval are the two constantly alternating elements in pulsation. Even though we usually find it easier to direct our listening and feeling toward perception of the pulse, it in fact only marks the *boundaries of intervals*. We can think of the interval as the immaterial aspect, the *soul*, so-to-speak, of a pulsation, while the pulse, corresponds to the material.

This rhythmic discovery was reaffirmed for me in Lao Tsu's statement about *space* which, of course, is another form of interval:

> Thirty spokes share the wheel's hub;
> It is the center hole that makes it useful.
> Shape clay into a vessel;
> It is the space within that makes it useful.
> Cut doors and windows for a room;
> It is the openings that make it useful
> Possession thus derives from what is there;
> Usefulness from what is not there...
>
> Lao Tsu, *Tao Te Ching*

Knowledge of the power of the interval affects my rhythmical development and my daily life in equal measure. The message that lives in the interval says: "You have time and space." I find it particularly helpful to remember this at stressful moments. Conventional time is only a construct of our mind, sometimes a force that makes our daily life seem rushed. When you enter the intervals of a pulsation deeper and deeper they lead you to timelessness, they guide you to a simultaneity of deep silence and pulsating movement.

A pulsation comes into being through the recurrence of *similar* events at *similar* intervals. That may sound very imprecise and we might be tempted to say: "Pulsation is the recurrence of *identical events at identical intervals.*"But I know of no instance in nature that pulsates with exactly equal intervals. The subtle fluctuation of your inner rhythm can be felt in your pulse. Within certain parameters, this inconsistency is not only a normal occurrence but an essential one as well in all naturally pulsating manifestations of life. But as soon as fluctuations within a pulsation exceed these parameters, the pulse becomes disrupted and we experience it as arhythmical. On the other hand, a pulsation with precisely regular intervals is experienced as being rigid and boring: the beats are no longer pulsating. Within every musician there exists both the measure of vital pulsation and the desire to play with as much rhythmic exactitude as possible. If those two poles are linked there appears both a great rhythmic stability and an exactitude with a perceptible flexibility.

There are several ways to symbolize or depict pulsation that make clear its essential nature. The following is derived from a walking movement:

This representation of pulsation appears linear but the essential nature of pulsation is *cyclic*. One of the main themes of this book is that all rhythmic phenomena may be experienced and understood as cyclic. Although Western *linear notation* facilitates comprehension of very complex musical relationships—both rhythmic and melodic structures. When music *sounds* the cyclic effect begins. Everything we experience in the energy-field of a cycle is perceived as a unity, therefore the appropriate visual image of a pulsation is a circle with an event at one point on its circumference. This event repeats itself time and again by way of an approximately regular movement on the circumference.

event

The event in an *audible* pulsation is a sound. We may imagine that this event involves a bell which sounds every time that point is reached.

acoustic event

Pulse and Beat

Pulse and beat are two different aspects of this acoustic event represented on the circumference. The beat is established actively, through our own creation, while the pulse occurs by itself just like our heartbeat. It is here that we meet two different spheres which are always interacting in music: the *inaudible* but *perceptible* rhythmic foundation as one sphere, and the *audible* rhythmic creations as the other. From this phenomenon we can develop two basic rhythmic abilities: the capacity to allow ourselves to be "carried along" while sensing the "inner pulse" and the ability to voluntarily shape the rhythm. Playing music, these two abilities are activated at one and the same time. How these two spheres may be experienced as a unified whole is covered in Section Four, "The Silent Pulse."

Beat and Off-Beat

Once you have become acquainted with pulse and interval as constantly alternating elements within a pulsation, you will encounter a new pair of opposites: beat and off-beat. When you establish a beat you will also hear its counterpart, like an echo at the mid-point of each interval. This is generally known as the *off-beat.* This term is, in fact, imprecise since everything which occurs away from the beat, throughout the interval, is "off-beat." Off-beat here is used to indicate the exact *mid-point* in an interval.

beat

offbeat

Clapping or playing the off-beat brings a new experience of the interval. In the following exercise, which requires a partner, you will gain practical experience of these characteristics of a pulsation: slight fluctuations within a vital pulse and the two elements of beat and off-beat.

> Sit opposite your partner, who should be allowed time to pre-pare for listening. Place a hand where you can feel your pulse and take all the time you need to feel it. Allow that heart pulsation to become audible by connecting each beat with a vocal sound. As soon as your partner can hear your voice, he or she begins to clap gently to the pulsation of your voice. Allow your partner enough time to follow the slight fluctuation in your pulse.
>
> When you hear your partner clap your vocal pulsation, gradu-ally remove your hand from the pulse and let your voice become ever quieter until only the pulsation clapped by your partner remains. Now your role is to listen. Gradually pay more attention to the mid-point of the interval. When you can hear the off-beats between your partner's clapping, allow them to become audible with your own clapping. Pay attention to the stability experienced in the give-and-take of your clapping and your partner's. After a while have your partner gradually accelerate. Allow yourself time to feel how the perception of the off-beat changes for you. As the clapping gets faster you will eventually reach a tempo which prevents you from follow-ing one another; feel how the beat and off-beat attract one another as the tempo increases.

The Silent Pulse

"If I clap my hands, it produces a sound. Can you show me the sound of one hand clapping?" This question, which a Zen Master once posed to his pupil, preoccupied me when I first heard it. Years later I was wandering through the mountains of Central Korea with a Zen monk. There were many temples in this barren but marvelously fascinating landscape which we tra-versed together. During the day, we roamed in silence through valleys and over mountain ridges and it seemed as if the chains of peaks and hills would never end. At night we would find a place to sleep in a temple.

One day, I asked my companion about the sound of one hand. Move-ment flickered in the monk's otherwise impassive face. We looked at one another for a long time, and he finally smiled but said nothing. Some days later, when we reached the monk's monastery, he took me into a small room where an old man with a strikingly erect posture was sitting. The almost palpable flexibility of his body and the clarity of his eyes made a strong impression on me. We sat facing one another in silence and I felt my sense of time changing. Time gradually came to a standstill. I don't know how long I sat like that in front of the old man, but a gesture from my companion, indicating that I should leave, suddenly brought me back to a world where time flows unceasingly onward. I left this small room with a deep bow. "The old man answered the question about the sound of one hand", the monk told me as we crossed the temple courtyard. "When his teacher demanded that he demonstrate the sound of one hand, his response was to slap the Master's face resoundingly."

That evening I sat on a meadow behind the temple and contemplated the events of the day. I was strangely moved by the amazingly simple solution to that problem, and the same question re-emerged from within myself in a new form. "If I clap with both hands I produce one beat. Can you show me the off-beat of that single beat?" A thousand thoughts, provoked by that question, buzzed through my head. How can there be an off-beat to a single beat? Where is the pulse to which this beat relates? If beat and off-beat coincide in a clap, would time stand still?

I looked up into the sky and in the dusk saw the moon as the stars grew ever brighter over Korea. All of a sudden it became clear: All around me is movement, and what I see in the sky are the manifestations of innumerable pulsations—the pulsation of the moon which envelops me even when it is not visible during the day; the pulsation of the earth which influences me even though at times I may not be aware of it. Then I started to hear the sound of crickets and frogs and I realized that I was surrounded by pulsations both audible and inaudible.

All at once the beat of my clap was related to all these pulsations which I hadn't perceived. The off-beat to my clapping could relate to any of these pulsations. But I also understood that I exist amid an endless diversity of ever-present pulsations. That very evening I had a presentiment that in all music there is the foundation of an inaudible, ever-present pulsation—*a silent pulse*.

When music becomes ever quieter and finally fades into silence, an *inaudible* and yet clearly *perceptible* pulsation persists for some time. This is the inaudible rhythmic foundation, *the silent pulse** in all music. We can call it a silent pulse because it is the inaudible but perceptible aspect in every form of music. We can, however, also call it the *inner pulse* since as soon as we hear music such a pulse arises within us. This is the pulse to which any musician listens for a couple of moments before he starts playing. By hearing within himself the music he is about to play, he connects with its silent pulse.

In this silent pulsation, the pulse and the interval are the two constant alternating elements. We experience that alternation as a succession of *heavy* and *light*. Heavy and light are relative qualities which can be felt as opposites. Any pulse produces within us a feeling of weight but we experience the interval as a light element. In a basic pulsation all the pulses are of equal weight. In the unfolding of a pulsation—as you will see in the next chapter—there can arise many nuances in the weight of a pulse.

The *audible* aspect of the silent pulse is created when the pulsation is manifested in sound. Whether it is clapped or played on an instrument, this
1   is the most elementary form of rhythmic expression. In Example 1, on the recording available as a supplement to this book, you can hear rhythm in this elementary form by way of a recording I made during my stay in a Korean Zen monastery. A monk plays the pulsation on a wooden block called a *moktak*, as an accompaniment to the singing. Notice how the pulsation of the *moktak* and the sound of the voices blend into a musical unity.

*I defer to general usage with the term silent pulse; a more accurate designation would be *silent pulsation*.

Moktak

The silent pulse is the foundation for rhythmic structure. When we sense that pulse, we can establish a relationship with any kind of music no matter how "unfamiliar" it may be. Even though we may not perceive every rhythmic quality, the sensing of a silent pulse creates a *bodily relationship*, an initial link, to new worlds of still unknown music.

If we stress the pulse, it gains more weight. But if we put the stress on the mid-point of the interval, the lighter element becomes more apparent. These two simple possibilities of structuring are the first presented herein. As you continue you will encounter many other possibilities. Each of these forms establishes a relationship of *creative tension* with the silent pulse. This pulse makes it possible to experience all rhythmic forms be they simple clapping or virtuoso playing.

16   In Example 16, you can experience the relationship of *audible* pulsation
and the *silent* pulse (pulsation). First you hear a simple pulsation played on
a *moktak* (heard in Example 1). This simple pulsation is embellished by various rhythmic figures on African bells called *gankogui*. Observe how the
pulsation of the wood-block remains perceptible even when it gradually
becomes quieter and finally vanishes completely. The audible pulsation thus
turns into a silent pulse, which is the rhythmic basis of everything heard. The
impact of the various bell figurations and the playing of the *dondo* (talking
drum) depends on their relationship to this perceptible but no longer audible pulsation. The silent pulse forms the musical context for rhythmic creativity. Audible pulsation and the silent pulse are two aspects of the most elementary rhythmic power.

Pulsation in the Realm of Sound

The discovery that we are surrounded by constant pulsations of all possible tempi raises these questions: What is the tempo range in which pulsations can provide a basis for musical creativity? What happens when an audible pulsation about as fast as your pulse accelerates? The faster a pulsation
becomes the more it approaches the state of *continuum*. At some point our
ear can no longer perceive the increasingly rapid sequence of pulses as separate entities. The pulses "unite" in our perception so that once a certain speed
has been attained we experience this audible pulsation as *a continuous tone*.
A slow pulsation then, forms the basis for musical rhythm but takes on a new
form as it becomes faster—it becomes *sound*.

Let's use our pulse as the basis for an audible pulsation. If we then create
a pulsation which is twice as fast, and synchronized with the first one, and
both are accelerating, a continuum will develop at some point. Once a certain speed is reached, we hear two tones which also vibrate in the ratio of
1:2, the sound of an octave. The pitch interval* of an octave is generated out
of the "double time" rhythmic relationship as the two pulsations become faster.

9   In Example 9, you can hear the sound of an octave and also of other pitch
intervals. This "transformation" of rhythmic ratios into pitch intervals also
applies to other rhythmic ratios (2:3, 3:4, 3:5, etc.) and is discussed further in
Chapter 5, Archetypes of Rhythm. An audible pulsation leaves the sphere of

*Pitch interval refers to the "distance" between two tones, and is measured in terms
of vibrational frequency whereas interval as used in this book refers to "space" or
distance between pulses sensed in terms of time.

musical rhythm at about 16 beats per second. This boundary is more than just an acoustical phenomenon since a musician's physiological capacity for fast playing also reaches its limit here. I've always been intrigued by this experiment: using a pulse of one second as a starting-point, I fill that space of one second with 2, then 3, 4, 5, 6, and finally more and more beats until I can't go any faster. As I do this over and over again my limits expand and various frequencies become recognizable *bodily feelings*.

In the Indian philosophy of music, rhythm and sound are one and the same fundamental energy which is expressed by the symbol for the primal sound "OM."

Indian mythology holds that music, in fact all existence, developed from the primal sound "OM." The upper part of the OM sign is called *Nada-Bindu*, which can be translated as Sound-Pulse. The semi-circle stands for sound, the feminine aspect of the world, which is embodied in Indian mythology by *Shakti*. The dot represents the pulse and corresponds to the male principle embodied by *Shiva*. Before the creation, *Shiva* and *Shakti* were an indissoluble whole. They hadn't yet recognized their polar manifestations and rested in a state of absolute stillness, representing a complete *absence* of vibration as well as *potential* vibration. Through the act of creation, however, they began to vibrate and appeared in their two forms, manifesting polarity: out of the energy of NADA, the sound, there developed tone intervals and melodies. BINDU, the pulsation in the slower sphere developed into the endless variety of musical rhythms. This pulsation became both the energy that fuels and the material that serves all musical rhythms.

Pulsation in the Slowest Realm of Musical Rhythm

If at a certain point, pulsations go beyond the realm of musical rhythms by accelerating, it seems reasonable to suppose that there is also a *lower* limit. Thus the question: What is the slowest pulsation which one can use as a basis for creating rhythms while playing with other people? During my first trip to Korea I was invited to take tea with Hwang Byung Ki, who is celebrated for his historical knowledge of Korean music. That trip was full of new discoveries for me and I noticed how impatient I became as the bus journey to Hwang Byung Ki's country home went on and on. I was eager to learn new things and viewed the time spent getting from one exciting distraction to another as an unfortunate necessity.

I was, therefore, all the more astonished when, after a brief, friendly greeting, Hwang Byung Ki suddenly asked me: "What, my friend, is the longest period of time we can experience together?" Before I had time to think about that he went to a jade slab hanging in a wonderfully decorated frame and struck it. When the sound died away, he struck it again, and invited me to

strike a bell in a similar frame in another corner of the room. At first, my concentration was totally directed toward the moment of striking, but then I noticed that it was considerably easier to make the next sound in unison with Hwang Byung Ki if I directed my attention toward the fading of the reverberations. Carried by these sounds, I was quickly submerged in a feeling of simultaneity and after a while I could feel the flow of my breathing synchronize with the fading of the reverberations.

Eventually, Hwang Byung Ki let the interval between the beats get longer and longer. I soon found it impossible to follow his playing. My fascination with the unity of sound and breathing vanished and I experienced an uneasiness similar to what I had felt during the bus ride. It had become impossible for me to *feel* the intervals between the beats, and the individual sounds followed one another without any sense of relationship. The question that Hwang Byung Ki once again put to me—in a slightly changed form—as we later had tea, is both simple and elemental: "What is the slowest pulsation we can use as a foundation for the creation of musical rhythm?"

That question leads us to the lower limit where pulsations leave the realm of music.

In the following exercise, you can experience how this limit is rooted in perception. You can try it with one or several partners.

> First, you establish a pulsation about the same as your pulse, with the syllables TA and KI. The others gradually take up your vocal pulsation until all the voices create a joint pulsation. When you give a previously agreed upon cue, everyone allows the vocal pulsation to become *half* as fast.

Voice	TA KI TA KI TA	KI	TA	KI
Pulsation	-O-O-O-O-O-O-O-O-O-O-O-O-			

> Give this cue several times and observe how long you and the others are able to sense the expanding intervals. Observe what you and your partners do in order ot feel such expanded periods of time. End the exercise when joint expression of pulsation becomes impossible.

In order to grasp intervals that become even longer, we usually embody the original pulsation by a foot or hand movement, or perhaps by nodding the head. After some time, however, the inevitable result is that we are no longer able to determine the increasing number of sub-dividing pulses. When we have lost that source of guidance, we are solely dependent on our subjective sense of time.

The time between two beats gets a new quality when it is experienced bodily. In this realm of very slow pulsations this is only possible with the assistance of a slow rhythmic movement, which exists already in our body. The flow of our breath is such a movement that allows us to experience long intervals as an undivided unity. With some practice, it is possible to synchronize the flow of your breath with that of other people so that it may become a bridge which links one pulse and the next at a very slow tempo. The simplest way of synchronizing the breath is to let it become audible vocally or instrumentally.

2   Audible breathing and my experience with Hwang Byung Ki provide the rhythmic basis for Example 2. This is the unfamiliar world of *Munmyochereak*—Chinese sacred music heard once a year at Seoul's Confucian temple. This music takes us into the slowest realm of pulsation. Two musicians sit in front of the p'yon'gyong and p'yon'jong (jade and bell chimes). Both instruments have the same tuning. Together the musicians play

a melody whose tones are temporally so far apart that they only seem to belong together if you are aware of how breathing fills the intervals. The flow of breath during such intervals is made audible by the *hun* and the *chi*, two wind instruments. Pulsations on which we can base musical rhythms are therefore limited to a certain tempo range. At the upper limit, we begin to hear individual pulses as a continuous sound or tone. At the lower tempo limit, the experience of long intervals can change in accordance with our subjective time feeling if a bodily point of reference is lacking.

Pulsation in the Body and in Other Natural Rhythms

The abundance of rhythms affecting us, however, extends beyond the limits of musical pulsations. Let's stay for a moment with the flowing of the breath. When the body is at rest, the breathing rhythm is flexibly related to the heartbeat. The heart beats between four and eight times during a breath cycle. If this rhythmic ratio varies beyond natural fluctuations, it is a sign that something is wrong. This rhythmic ratio is normally an expression of our psychological and physical harmony. As we breathe, the two nostrils do not always function equally. More air flows through one than the other. An alternation occurs every two hours in the case of a healthy person. People generally breathe through one nostril at a time as the tissue expands slightly in the other—a rhythm involving the two halves of our body.

After a period of activity, we need rest or sleep. Of course it is possible to deliberately prolong the phases of activity, but there comes a point when we must relinquish our waking awareness in order to submerge ourselves for a time in a state of dream and sleep consciousness. Normally, we are awake during the day and sleep at night. Investigations of subterranean life-rhythms have, however, shown that our sleep-rhythms are independent of the change between light and dark. When isolated in a cave, the human organism starts to live a rhythm that corresponds to the 24.8 hours of a lunar day. That is a rhythm which only approximates 24 hours and is therefore called circadian (*circa*: about, *dies*: day). In her book *Body Time*, Gay Gaer Luce writes:

> If we were abandoned in a salt mine with some food and entertainment, we would settle down to a circadian cycle of activity and rest—although we might oscillate at first. The circadian cycle seems to be an important organizing principle in our physiology. People may be unaware that their body temperature, blood pres-

sure, respiration, pulse, blood sugar, hemoglobin levels and amino acid levels rise and fall in circadian cycles. So do our adrenal hormones, our urine volume, and almost every function from the rate of cell division to mood. Many rhythms go unnoticed. For instance, the skin temperature, particularly of the hands and feet, changes in a circadian rhythm.

As I was writing this book, a number of experiments with my sleeping and waking rhythms developed of their own accord. I increasingly wrote at night in order to work in peace. Finally, I was getting up at dusk and going to bed at dawn. It was winter so I had the long nights for undisturbed work and after more than a month of that I felt bright and healthy. I was living, so-to-speak, on the *off-beat* of my usual life-rhythm. When it became apparent that I was experimenting with my life-rhythm, I started deliberately shifting, by one hour, the time I rose and retired. During this phase, I had difficulty falling asleep and also felt increasingly tired. It seemed as if my inner rhythm was gradually becoming disoriented. Finally I yielded to the imminent chaos, allowing my periods of sleeping and waking to become completely arbitrary. I was struck by how quickly I reached a threatening state of existential confusion: a momentarily racing pulse, depressive states, and constant tension were clear signs that it was time to return to a regular rhythm. Overall I slept almost as much as usual, so the amount of sleep was not the crucial factor. Much more important was the inner need for a rhythm regulating waking consciousness and those states of self-awareness during sleep. A rhythmic alternation between different states and levels of consciousness seems to be vitally necessary for human beings.

The further apart events within a pulsation are, the more difficult it becomes to recognize them as recurring elements. For someone who lives in the country, the phases of the moon are still very much part of everyday reality and for many women the lunar rhythm is clearly linked with their menstrual cycle. We find the impact of the moon's rhythmically changing gravitational pull in tidal movements and as the moon waxes, plant shoots grow faster while the roots proliferate as the moon wanes. The pulsing of a distant celestial body thus connects to the more rapid pulsations in and around us. Pulsation is the primal force behind the diverse phenomena of sound, rhythm, planetary movement and much more. Events in one sphere are reflected in another. Musical rhythm is therefore a reflection of the rhythm in nature. The experience of musical pulsation thus provides us with direct access to *all* the phenomena associated with pulsation.

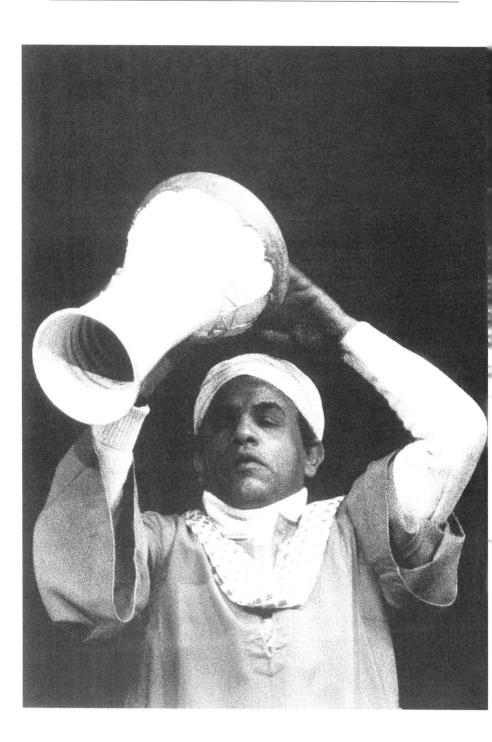

4

THE UNFOLDING AND DEVELOPMENT OF PULSATION

I n the first elementary exercises of this book you experienced pulsation in different ways with your body, and learned about various possibilities and aspects of that primal rhythmic energy. As you ponder the endless variety of rhythms that exist in this world, you might now ask these questions: What is the connection between these complex forms of rhythm and the simplicity of a pulsation? Does a pulsation develop into new rhythmic forms of its own accord, or is the unfolding of a pulsation created by the musician? As we have already seen, both cases apply. Musicians simply recreate the rhythmic processes already existing by mirroring the beauty and magic of the rhythmic laws in nature. I will try to show how these laws, present since the beginning of our universe, and the musical creations developed by individuals over time, are interrelated.

The Interaction of Rhythmic Movements

Rhythmic movements influence each other whenever they come into a field of contact. Two pendulums, for example, swinging next to each other, will start to synchronize their movements after some time. This is a law of nature. Or, imagine the following situation: A number of people are walking in the same room and are aware of their footsteps. They walk at different speeds so you will naturally hear and feel many different pulsations occurring simultaneously. It may be that initially you hear two walking pulsations that seem to have no relationship at all. After some time, the people gradually start to combine each footsetp with a gentle sound of the voice which expresses their own walking rhythm. Soon you will hear more and more people synchronizing their footsteps in various ways: some will join in the same pulsation, others will meet with their steps in halftime or doubletime or other relationships.

I have often tried this simple experiment and found that people will always tend to synchronize their walking rhythms in one way or another. But it also eventually happens that some people, for whatever reason, voluntarily resist the process of synchronization and stay with their own walking rhythm. This shows that synchronization is dependent upon both voluntary and involuntary rhythmic movement. On the one hand, we can voluntarily tune into a specific rhythm, on the other hand, we can avoid the natural tendancy of synchronization altogether. An involuntary rhythmic movement, however, moving on its own accord, will always have the tendency to synchronize with other movements. Synchronization is a law of nature that shows the great variety of contact possibilities between different rhythmic movements. In this process, the pulses attract each other and the energy fields of the intervals tend to fuse or meet each other in simple relationships.

In two random pulsations, it can happen that no pulses coincide over a long period of time. The following graphic shows two pulsations with very few points of contact:

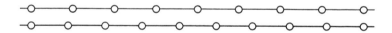

Only after 8 pulses in the upper pulsation and 9 pulses in the lower pulsation, will two pulses occur simultaneously. But as the process of synchronization occurs, the pulsations will fuse in an increasing number of pulses. The synchronization could lead to a complete melting together of both pulsations. They are then identical. But there are also a number of other possibilities to which the mutual influence might lead. You will learn more about the complex ways of synchronization later in this book. For now, let's look at how a certain pulsation synchronizes with another one in two simple ways:

1) The original pulsation is *faster* than the additional pulsation. The slower pulsation meets every second, third, fourth, etc. pulse of the original pulsation. This coincidence of pulses creates *emphasis*, thus grouping the pulses in the original pulsation. The following illustration shows this process:

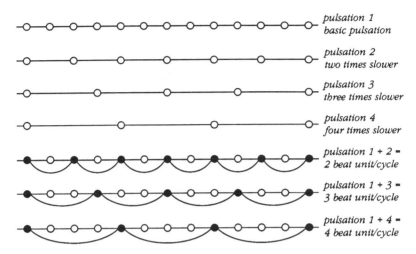

The *combining of pulses* into coherent groups creates *units;* recurrence of the unit gives us the *cycle.* A *unit* creates a sense of belonging together, while *cycle* refers to recurrence. Nonetheless both *unit* and *cycle* are simply different aspects of the same thing; that is, the *grouping of pulses.*

2) The original pulsation is *slower* than the additional pulsation. When both pulsations synchronize, a *division of the intervals* in the orginal pulsation is created. The original pulsation will then exhibit a new quality and sound different depending on how many sub-dividing pulses are audible or perceptible in each interval. The following illustration shows this process:

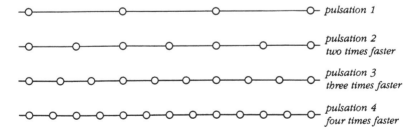

Here is the original pulsation in various divisions:

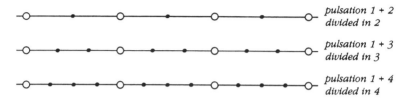

pulsation 1 + 2
divided in 2

pulsation 1 + 3
divided in 3

pulsation 1 + 4
divided in 4

The Combining of Pulses

The Grouping of Pulses: A Perceptive Tendancy

Beat and offbeat are polarities and can be visually represented on opposite sides of the circle. Within such a circle all possible polarities may appear:

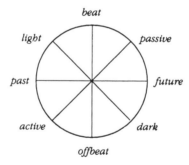

The tension, both attraction and repulsion, between polarities enables us to experience the moving power of Being. In our body for example, we experience polarity as differences of expression between our left and right side, left and right brain functions, the flowing in and out of the breath, and the interaction of systole and diastole in the beating of the heart.

When sensing a slow pulsation we find the same polarity in the alternation of pulse and interval. As a pulsation becomes faster the intervals become shorter, causing the pulses to move into the foreground of our perception. As the tempo increases we eventually reach a point where the sense of polarity between pulse and interval disappears. We tend to re-establish this lost polarity by an act of "creative hearing": a regular sequence of:

	TAK	TAK	TAK	TAK...		
may be perceived as	TIK	TAK	TIK	TAK...		
or even	TIK	TAK	TAK	TIK	TAK	TAK...

Since we all react this way it's clear to me that creative hearing is a natural function of human consciousness; this way of grouping pulses seems to occur involuntarily. We can, however, voluntarily combine several pulses. In the simplest case, two successive beats seem to belong together if we stress every other beat. We then hear a succession of two-beat units. We can achieve the same effect by an alternation of two different sounds or pitches. Playing in this manner allows us to easily hear the units, but it will lack rhythmic creativity.

The Weight Pattern

In music, the audible and the inaudible constantly affect each other. Every rhythmic form spontaneously establishes an inaudible rhythmic ground. No matter how complex the sound and rhythm created by a drum may be, it always implies the inaudible foundation which enables us to hear the grouping of pulses. We sense this inaudible foundation as a succession of pulses which *vary in weight.* Unlike an accent which is imposed, the weight is a pulse quality that occurs by itself. It is a result of the pulse's position within the *weight pattern*, a term I use for the unfolding of the silent pulse.

Audible Aspect:	*Inaudible Aspect:*
Pulsation	Silent Pulse
Cycle	Weight Pattern

We base our rhythmic creations on the weight pattern and from each creation there arises a specific weight pattern; this is how the audible and inaudible realms are interrelated.

We can create rhythms by using a variety of accents, by varying the drum sound itself, and creating diverse intervals which work either in harmony with, or in opposition to, the basic pulsation. Later on we'll examine drum sound variation and diverse intervals. For now, let's remember that an accent is something we impose whereas we feel the weight as a naturally occurring pulse quality in a cycle. A knowledge of the principles of units and cycles is derived from two sources: our predisposition for "creative hearing" and the laws of vibration as they apply to rhythmic movement. These laws are explored more fully in Chapter Five.

Two Beats as Unit and Cycle

When a pulsation becomes synchronized with another that is moving at half its speed, every other pulse will be reinforced and thereby gain more weight.

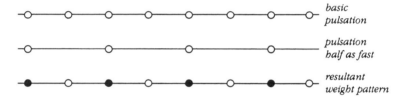

The heavy pulse followed by a lighter one then forms a unit of two *related beats*. Of course, repetition of this unit without change creates a cycle as well. The following illustration represents this cyclical aspect.

There are a number of ways of experiencing the weight pattern of a two-beat unit through bodily movement. We can use either an up and down or a side to side movement, but the important thing is that you feel the different weight of each pulse. With the following exercise, I invite you to take part in this experience. Do this in a way that feels right to you and let every individual phase take as long as it needs.

Begin in a standing position. Close your eyes, and take time to visualize the inner space of your body. Sense how the soles of your feet touch the ground, and feel the area between your soles and the highest point of the skull. The ankles, knees, pelvis, shoulders, and neck are different levels within that space. Play with those levels until you are standing straight and upright without strain. By gently swaying backward and forward and from side to side with your whole body, you can find the center point between front and back, left and right. Observe how you feel the displacement of weight in the soles of your feet. Let your movements gradually become less until you sense that your body weight rests equally on the heels, balls of the feet and toes.

Now put your hand where your pulse can be felt. This could be on the neck, wrist or abdomen. Allow yourself time to feel your heartbeat become perceptible there, and gradually let the pulse become audible by joining a vocal "TA" with each pulse. For a while, follow the fluctuations of the pulse with your voice. Then allow the pulsation of your voice to become gradually more regular and when you're ready, remove your hand from the pulse. Make sure that the pulsation of your voice persists. When you feel ready, bend the knees slightly with every TA, and straighten them during the interval between each TA. Feel your entire body start a relaxed and flowing up and down movement. As you bend the knees to every TA, you move downward a little. When you straighten your knees during the intervals, you move up again. While you are doing that, remember how you stood upright and the feeling of the center-point between front and back, left and right. Sense how this up and down movement becomes more firmly established as the sound of your voice becomes completely one with the movement.

When you feel ready, change your vocalization to an alternation of TA and KI. Intensify your downward movement on the TA and let the downward movement on KI become smaller and lighter. Feel how these two successive downward movements differ in intensity. After some time, allow your movements to become ever smaller, and your voice quieter. Can you sense in your knees the difference between the two downward movements, even though they are greatly diminished? When your voice has become inaudible and your movements so reduced that you can hardly feel them, you will sense within yourself a weight pattern wherein two successive pulses differ in weight.

There are two possibilities for making the succession of heavy and light audible on a drum. The first is to stress the heavy pulse while leaving the lighter pulse unaccented. For example, you could play the full, open sound of a bass drum on the heavy pulse and leave the lighter pulse free, or play a gentle, muffled sound; the accent on the heavy pulse gives it a greater weight while the free or softer pulse becomes even lighter. The second possibility is a reversal of the weight pattern: the heavy is unaccented or given a lighter accent, while the lighter one is stressed which moves it toward the center of attention. If you play these two possibilities on a bass drum, you hear the foundation of two "contrary" rhythms. Stress on the heavy element gives us the rhythmic basis of the *march*; accentuation of the lighter element produces the basis of the *samba.*

The bass drum used for a march is a cylindrical wooden drum with two membranes. This drum is struck with a beater so that the membrane vibrates undampened and causes the other skin to resonate. The bass drum beat in a *march* occurs on the heavy pulse and causes a feeling of heaviness to dominate. The bass drum used in the Brazilian *samba* is known as the *surdo* and is also a cylindrical drum. The player carries it in front of him so he can dampen the upper membrane with his hand; he uses the full, undampened sound of the bass drum on the lighter pulse.

The self-assertiveness of the *march* is evident in the way the feet firmly strike the ground. We feel its movement within us even though we may be standing still. This inner movement is a downward flow of energy which expresses , through the body, such things as the desire to impress or a show of force.

Listening to a *samba,* we experience a peculiar rhythmic phenomenon; since we normally feel the heavy beat as the beginning of a unit, the samba seems to counter that effect because it stresses the second beat of the unit. In Example 3, you can hear the different rhythmic foundations for the *march* and the *samba.* "Vençeremos," a song from the Chilean liberation movement, may not sound like a typical march, but it is based on a march rhythm. Following that is a *samba de roda* (pronounced: hoda), an original form of the *samba* from Salvador/Bahia. The singing lets you hear the actual flow of heavy and lighter pulses and the beginning of every two-beat unit. The *surdo* provides a contrast to that flow. Only in the entire context, does the playing of the surdo take effect because without the singing and other instruments, we would soon start to perceive the rhythm in reverse. We would then feel the undampened boom of the surdo as the first beat. In a *march,* the reinforcement of the heavy pulse creates weightiness but the *samba* generates a feel-

3

ing of lightness and vitality which we find wherever the weight pattern is polarized as previously described.

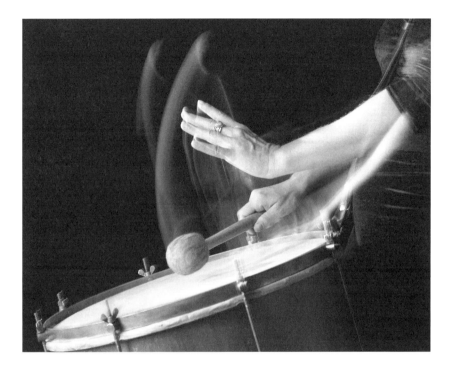

Surdo

In the *samba de roda* from Example 3, you also hear the sound of a *berimbão*, an Afro-Brazilian musical bow that I use in TA KE TI NA workshops. In addition to its rhythmic impact, the *berimbão* produces a drone which invites one to sing and although it's a simple instrument, a skillful player can create many interesting sounds on it. A string *(corda)* is stretched end to end on a biriba branch *(vara)* and to that is tied a gourd *(cabaça)* which functions as a resonator. The player strikes the string with a thin rod *(vaqueta)* and also holds a little rattle *(caxixi)* in the same hand. Between the thumb and index finger of the other hand the player holds a stone *(lapis)* or a coin *(dobrão)* which he uses to vary the string sound. By pressing firmly on the string a higher sound is produced but if the string is touched lightly with the stone we hear a rasping percussive sound. Four different rhythms thus come together as one: the rhythm of the *caxixi*, the sound of the open and the divided string, the rasping sounds and the various sounds produced by moving the *cabaça* toward and away from the body.

Berimbão

The *berimbão* originated in Africa and was brought by slaves to Salvador/Bahia where it became the main instrument of the *Capoeira*, a discipline which links dance, poetry, music and self-defense. This practice helped the blacks survive the inhumanities of colonialism by providing a means for expressing feelings and physical self-defense.

Three Beats as Unit and Cycle

When we project a "melody" (such as TIK TAK or TIK TAK TAK) or other forms of accentuation onto a regular pulsation, we usually combine pulses into two or three beat units. These two groupings are the basic *compound pulses.* Their energy is so fundamentally different that we can think of them as "contrary." This accounts for the entirely different effect a *march* has in contrast to that of a *waltz.* This effect holds true for all music based on two and three beat cycles.

When a random pulsation meets another pulsation moving three times slower, and is synchronized with it, *three* pulses then combine to form a unit.

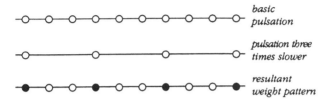

basic
pulsation

pulsation three
times slower

resultant
weight pattern

The joint impact of the two pulsations strengthens the common beat and gives every third pulse greater weight. Repetition of this weight pattern creates a three-beat cycle.

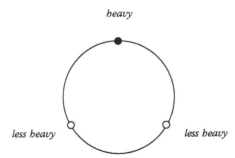

heavy

less heavy   *less heavy*

The following exercise enables you to experience the weight pattern of a three-beat unit:

> Begin by walking at about the same rate as your pulse. Take your time so that you can clearly sense the pulsation of your movement. Gradually add your voice by setting down your right foot to the sound of TA and your left foot to KI. When you feel that the pulsation of your voice has united with that of your walking, let your forward movement become ever smaller until you are walking in place. When you are ready, switch from TA KI to the three syllables: GA MA LA. Each step is still accompanied by one syllable. Notice that GA MA LA starts first on one foot and then on the other. Gradually direct more attention to the syllable GA.

Now put each foot that steps with the syllable GA, a bit forward
so that the side to side movement of your steps expands into a "triangle." Gradually also add your body-weight to the forward step.
Observe how your upper body is brought into this movement. Again
allow yourself time for the movements to become smaller and smaller
and your voice ever quieter. How small can you make the "triangle"
and still perceive it? Let your voice gradually become inaudible but
continue hearing the syllables mentally and reduce your movements
until you can hardly sense the "triangle." Now you can feel the flow
of three-beat cycles within yourself and, if you like, you can use Example 11 as an accompaniment.

11

Externalizing a three beat cycle such as you have just experienced gives
us the basic rhythm of the *waltz*. If you listen carefully to a *waltz* you'll notice that the first beat of every *four* cycles is given additional emphasis. This
lends the *waltz* its characteristic "floating" quality. Here we have a rhythmic
movement which is larger than its individual components. This leads us into
a new realm, one of longer rhythmic periods and cycles. In non-European
cultures, we find many rhythms based on three-beat cycles which are what
we might call the "opposite" of the *waltz*. Here the stress appears on the
second and *third* beat while the first is either lighter or not played at all. But
no matter what the rhythmic structure may be, the weight pattern of the three-
beat cycle is perceived in the same way by all people, regardless of their
culture.

The Difference Between Unit and Cycle

As we discovered earlier, a unit is a group of pulses that are brought
together by a difference in pulse weight. In the cycle, however, the most
important aspect is its *recurrence* and its point of reference is the first beat
which marks the end of a cycle as well as the beginning of a new one. If the
weight pattern of a two beat unit repeats itself without change then the unit
itself is also a cycle. This, however, is not always the case: when two *unequal* units appear in succession such as a two-beat unit followed by one of
three-beats, both units lose their individual cyclical character. They then become elements in a larger *five-beat cycle*. As you see, a larger cycle is formed
through the succession of two units of unequal size. That leads us to these
questions: what is the influence of short and long elements on a pulsation?
What other ways of synchronization are still to be experienced?

Recitative Rhythms

Up to this point, we have considered pulsation to be the foundation and origin of rhythmic movement. But certainly not all of life's manifestations are based on a regularly recurrent pulsation. The rhythmic expression of our speech is not carried by a regular pulsation; it is created by the succession of long and short elements which are derived from the meaning of the word itself. If we speak the word "music" so that it consists of two short components, it begins to lose its meaning. The succession of a long and a short element constitutes this word's "recitative rhythm." Without that, the meaning of the word is not transmitted.

We clarify our language by way of bodily gestures so that the person we are talking to can perceive not only the meaning of our words but also react to the rhythmic shape of our speech, and to the "dance" which underlies it. A long pause in the right place endows what is said with space and significance. On the other hand, a momentary acceleration of the flow of speech makes a long arc of words more comprehensible. Neither *long* nor *short* has a specific temporal value. Long and short are the succession of two time elements perceptibly different in length. Both are to be experienced as opposites and only take on a time value relative to each other.

Tschangdan is the Korean word for rhythm. Translated literally, it means "long - short." Asymmetry and the interaction of long and short elements are to be found in all aspects of Korean rhythm. KUNG (with a drawn-out "u") and TOK (with a short "o") are examples of long and short sounds. They form a free rhythmic gesture, which I have often encountered in Korean dances and music.

kung   *tok*

The interplay of long and short is the rhythmic foundation of speech and I call this free shaping of rhythm with no regular pulsation, *recitative rhythm.*

The Impact of Recitative Rhythms on a Pulsation

Recitative rhythms and pulsative rhythms are separate worlds, each existing on its own but often coming into contact as, for instance, when an African storyteller presents a tale to the gentle pulse of his drum. The two worlds often feed on one another, forming combinations. The free rhythmic vocalization of KUNG-TOK produces a succession of long and short. If these enter the energy-field of a pulsation, indefinite intervals come into contact with a regular succession of equal intervals. If they synchronize, the result will be a succession of two units varying in size. In the simplest case, the long element will combine two pulses, and the short one pulse. Through repetition, the two different elements become perceptible as a whole.

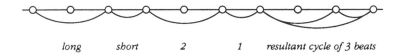

long   short   2   1   resultant cycle of 3 beats

This perceptible unity includes three successive beats. The weight pattern, however, makes this unit different from the one you've already encountered. In both three-beat units, the greatest weight is on the first beat, but when a long and a short coincide with a pulsation as described there is an additional emphasis on the third beat. This creates a weight pattern with three different nuances.

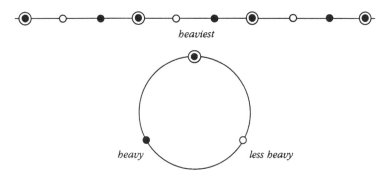

You can make the three-beat cycle audible by using the following speech rhythm. Its character will become clear to you by clapping more loudly on TA and less loudly on TIT.

Clap   O · O O · O O · O
Voice   TA KI TIT TA KI TIT TA KI TIT

This is the simplest way of creating units within a pulsation using long and short values. Since neither a long nor a short has a specific time value, a long element can be given three beats while the short can receive *two* beats. This creates two units of different lengths. In this sequence the three and two beat units are elements in a greater whole and their alternation produces a five-beat cycle. As always, this will become perceptible through the cycle's weight pattern. The first beats of both units now differ in weight. The first beat of the three-beat unit is the heaviest since both that unit and the entire cycle begin there.

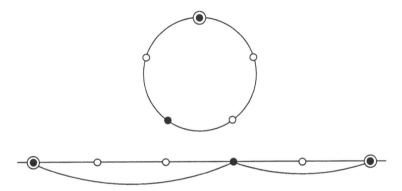

Tsching

4   Use recorded Example 4 to experience this five-beat cycle. It begins with the vocal rhythm:

Voice   GA MA LA TA KI GA MA LA TA KI

You also hear the "*tsching*," a Korean gong marking each GA LA and TA.

Tsching   ◇ · ◆ ◇ · ◇ · ◆ ◇ ·
Voice   GA MA LA TA KI GA MA LA TA KI
                 ◇ = *open sound of tsching*   ◆ = *dampened sound of tsching*

First, speak this rhythm and notice the *moktak* as it stresses the first syllable in each unit. The *moktak* indicates in almost all the recorded examples the syllables that coincide with the clapping.

Clap   ○ · · ○ · ○ · · ○ ·
Voice   GA MA LA TA KI GA MA LA TA KI

Allow yourself time to sense the simple flow of the five-beat cycle. To begin with, you'll hear me vocalize various combinations of the two syllables TIN and GO while the clapping continues without change. You may try to respond to this vocal rhythm by repeating it aloud. Make sure that your clapping keeps to the same simple flow. Only in relation to the clapping do the TIN - GO variations become rhythmically meaningful. If when responding you sometimes lose the clapping or the rhythmic orientation, listen again for a while to the simple GA MA LA TA KI which is always heard in the background. At the end of this example, other instruments enter, shaping the five-beat cycle in various ways. Continue clapping the cycle and notice that the GA MA LA TA KI always remains as the foundation for the rhythmic development.

The use of successive long and short units creates the multi-faceted world of *additive cycles*, to which we will return later in this chapter. A unit which is the result of superimposition of two or more pulsations differs from those brought about by the interaction of long-short and a pulsation. Superimposition of two pulsations creates a cycle comprised of *equal parts*, whereas long and short units in succession create one of *unequal parts* and thus, a more complex cycle.

The Subdivision of the Interval

The interval is the "soul" of pulsation. Like any empty space the interval has the potential for dividing itself in certain ways. Whenever new pulses appear in the original empty space the quality of the pulsation is immediately changed. As we used the circle to represent a cycle so can we use it as an image for the recurrent interval. The circle itself symbolizes *wholeness*.

pulse

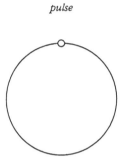

When the interval, symbolized by a circle, is divided into three equal parts it is neither smaller nor larger than the original entity, but it is different. It exhibits a new quality, one which relates directly to the laws governing vibrating strings, wood, metal, air columns and so on, because an interval between two pulses reacts exactly like an air column or a string. When a string is set into motion, it produces several tones simultaneously but we are usually aware of only one of these. That one is the lowest and it is called the *fundamental*. Once it begins to vibrate the string divides itself into shorter sections which give out higher tones known as *overtones* or *harmonics*. These harmonics can be heard clearly by gently touching the vibrating string at a point that divides the string into halves, thirds, quarters, and so on. Every point produces a different tone. This phenomenon has an exact corollary in the world of rhythm: the rhythmic *quality* of an interval varies according to the number of its subdivisions. Thus, an interval divided into three equal parts feels entirely different than one divided into two equal parts. We will examine this important phenomenon more closely in Chapter 5, Archetypes of Rhythm.

5   In Example 5, you can feel the impact of a given interval change as the number of subdivisions changes.

> First, listen to the vocal rhythms, paying attention to how one and the same interval changes its impact, depending on the various speech rhythms. Next, you can try to speak the speech rhythms yourself. To do that, first establish a pulsating walk, keeping step with the *surdo* on the recording. With this pulsating walk you will feel the intervals physically. Now, try to speak the individual rhythm words when the *berimbāo* replaces the syllables and provides you with rhythmic support. (See opposite page.)

The various divisions of the interval are shown here in a linear form so as to establish the relationship with walking. It is easy to see that additional syllables fill the intervals of the basic pulsation at every change of speech rhythm. What, in the diagram, looks like a mathematical division of space, can be experienced in the recorded example as a succession of different rhythmic qualities. The increasing *quantity* of syllables thereby creates a different rhythmic *quality*. Of course, the tempo of a pulsation determines how many subdividing pulses are musically meaningful in the interval. It is often the case that no additional beats are possible in rhythms based on a very fast pulsation. At slow tempi, on the other hand, a continuous change of color in an otherwise constant rhythm occurs when the subdivisions are varied.

My experience with various rhythmic traditions has revealed an interesting tendency regarding the impact of subdividing pulsations. Rhythms that have GA MA LA in the subdividing pulsations make the listener more introverted and bring him or her toward an inner stillness, whereas the intervals containing the movement of TA KI or TA KE TI NA will direct the listener toward outer movement and greater extroversion.

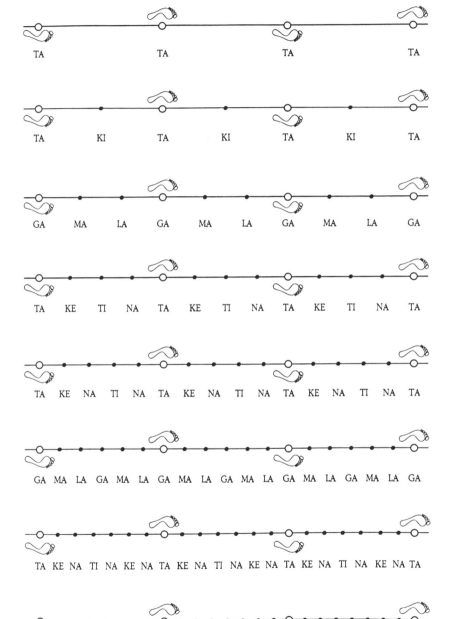

The Five Elementary Off-Beats

As I have previously mentioned, the *entire interval* is "off-beat". The individual off-beats under consideration here are different echoes of the beat. All off-beats occur on one or the other of the various sub-divisions of a pulsation. When regular movement of a sub-dividing pulsation becomes inaudible and only one of these pulses remains, an off-beat is created.

There are five elementary off-beats which are found as rhythmic building blocks in the music of all cultures. You already know the simplest: the echo of the beat, right at the interval's mid-point. This "off-beat" occurs exactly opposite the beat:

beat

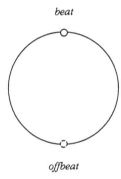

offbeat

In the sub-dividing pulsation employing the syllables TA KE TI NA, this off-beat falls exactly on TI. But alongside the TI, there are also the KE and NA as subdividing pulses. These are not directly opposite the beat. They are considerably closer to the beat than the simple off-beat. This gives them a tendency to fuse with the beat, and we experience them as being much more charged with tension than the off-beat. Their position seems to be much more unstable than that of the off-beat. Experience shows that they are more difficult to find than the simple off-beat when attempting to clap them for the first time. The circle shows the relationship between KE, NA, and the beat.

TA

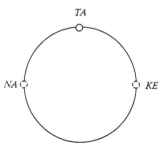

KE and NA are off-beats in a pulsation twice as fast as the original so they are called *"double-time off-beats."*

The two off-beats yet to be considered are found in the GA MA LA sub-division. They divide the interval into three parts. It's easy to see that together with the beat they form a triangle inside the circle. This triangle seems to exert a stabilizing influence since most people can usually clap the GA MA LA off-beats much more easily than the double-time off-beats.

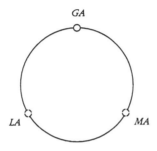

The off-beats of the GA MA LA sub-division are frequently used in the various world rhythms. As previously mentioned, there are also other off-beats in addition to the five basic ones. These derive from the faster sub-divided pulsations which you hear in Example 5. In addition to the five elementary off-beats, you will also hear two more combinations from the GA MA LA GA MA LA sub-division in Example 6.

6

Use Example 6 to discover the quality of the five elementary off-beats. Maybe some of what is happening on the recording is too fast for you. After you've heard how the various off-beats sound, you can practice them at your own tempo and for as long as you like by using clapping, voice, and steps without the recording.

First, start walking in time with the foot-rattle and the sound of the *surdo*. At the same time, follow the recording and use your voice to sub-divide each interval within your pulsating walking with the four syllables TA KE TI NA. The *moktak* first plays the elementary off-beat at the midpoint of the interval. Try to clap with each beat of the *moktak* while your walking and vocal rhythm remain unchanged. The off-beat falls on the TI of your vocal rhythm. In this piece you will again hear various improvisations (TIN - GO) in vocal rhythm to which you may respond. The important thing is that your clapping and walking should continue unchanged. Even though you change to the improvised syllables you continue to feel the TA KE TI NA within you. There thus develops a new rhythmic level, which sometimes supports the clapping and sometimes rhythmically confronts your walking and clapping. Allow yourself time to speak the vocal rhythms, and observe how they affect the flow of your walking.

Later, the *moktak* changes from the syllable TI to KE. When you clap with the *moktak* and your steps match the *surdo*, you will experience the rhythmic energy of a *double-time off-beat*.

It may be that you can clap both KE and NA effortlessly. If you feel it is a strain to clap the double-time off-beat, return to simply walking. If you're straining, you may manage to clap the double-time off-beat a few times, but you won't come in contact with its energy. The more time you allow yourself to listen, the quicker the various off-beats will become familiar.

In the second part of the recording, the speech rhythm changes to GA MA LA. With this sub-division of the pulsation, you will become familiar with the off-beats on MA and LA. As before, step with the surdo while clapping to the *moktak* if you can manage without straining.

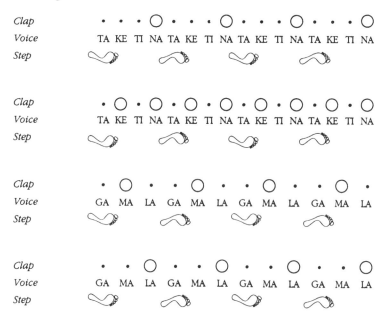

The rhythmic path of TA KE TI NA allows us to experience the off-beats as specific bodily feelings. Repeated experience anchors such movement in your consciousness. Off-beats thus become rhythmic building blocks with which you can play at any time. This is the beginning of the way taken by TA KE TI NA. First you become familiar with the supportive power of a pulsation. This provides a rhythmic ground and offers the sense of being carried. Next comes the experience of the various cycles and rhythmic intervals. And finally, bodily comprehension of the off-beat enables the gathering of rhythmic building blocks, which come together in a great range of combinations to form rhythmic figures. Once you have reached that point, the ground has been prepared for rhythmic creativity.

Twelve Is Sixteen

My involvement with non-European rhythms began in India. While there, I found teachers and masters who were not only concerned with technique but, for whatever reason, seemed to know my inner preoccupations of the moment. Studying under tabla master Ustad Mohamed Ahmed Khan, I quickly observed that his way of teaching drew me into a vortex of inner experiences. I visited him every evening and we sat down together for my lesson. He would spend hours teaching me how to play one particular sound on the tabla, and still would not be satisfied, even if I, with the best will in the world, couldn't hear any difference between his sound and mine. Other times, he would play long rhythmic compositions for me, and then demand that I repeat them. But I couldn't understand what he had played, and didn't receive the slightest explanation to help me recognize the structure in his pieces.

Nevertheless, it was I, not he, who was upset by the fact that for hour upon hour I was incapable of grasping so much as the beginning of what he had just played. With a tranquil smile, he played the same piece over and over again. My only orientation was to count the basic beats so that I could at least discover which cycles he was playing. But when Mohamed Ahmed Khan discovered my counting, he laughed derisively: "Why don't you use a computer?"

One evening he told me that I had learned enough and was ready to learn a longer rhythmic composition. He wanted to teach me a *Quayada in*

Teental—a rhythmic composition with a *sixteen*-beat cycle. He started to play, and I, with all my attention, attempted to follow him. I was completely absorbed in his playing when, after a while, I realized that his tabla figurations were repeated after *twelve* beats. That confused me and I didn't know whether Mohamed Khan was putting me to the test, or whether I simply couldn't understand the connection with *sixteen* beats. Finally I gave voice to my perplexity, and interrupted his playing: "I don't understand your composition, Baba. What I hear is a *twelve-beat* cycle; I can't find a *sixteen-beat* cycle." He looked up, gazed questioningly at me, and said: "What do you mean? *Twelve IS sixteen!*" And with that he dismissed me for the evening.

I went back toward the little room I had near the Bombay Central Station, past the crowd of people on the street already set up for the night. I hardly saw anything. All I could feel was despair over my inability to understand. It was clear to me that something was right about what Mohamed Khan had said, but the same picture kept reappearing before my eye:

```
1   2   3   4   5   6   7   8   9   10  11  12
•———•———•———•———•———•———•———•———•———•———•———•
equals
1   2   3   4   5   6   7   8   9   10  11  12  13  14  15  16
•———•———•———•———•———•———•———•———•———•———•———•———•———•———•———•
```

12=16...   12=16...   12=16...

It was impossible for me to sleep, so I sat in front of my tabla. Where should I start, and if I couldn't make sense of it, what was the point of all this practice? I stroked the skin of the tabla and hit it, simply wanting to hear its sound. And out of this "playing around" there came the simplest flow of sixteen beats that I knew:

DHA	DHIN	DHIN	DHA
DHA	DHIN	DHIN	DHA
DHA	TIN	TIN	TA
TETE	DHIN	DHIN	DHA...

How often, in the past, that flow of sixteen beats had established itself in my playing. My thoughts calmed down and finally ceased altogether as the rhythmic movement on the tabla became audible and gradually cast its spell over me. I sensed ever more clearly the first beat. Then I felt within myself a circular movement growing stronger and stronger. It gave me a strange, exciting feeling, unlike any I had ever experienced. But as I continued to play, I grew more and more tired and finally fell into a deep sleep...

I soon found myself standing on an endless plain watching long columns of strange number-like creatures march past me. Their faces were all different, they looked sad and exhausted. They bore heavy burdens, and they emanated a feeling of hopelessness. I couldn't see where they came from or where they were going. These creatures never even looked at one another. Nonetheless, rank after endless rank moved toward some unknown objective. I felt alone, afraid, and wanted to scream, but I couldn't. I wanted to run away to another world but I was unable to move.

The plain slowly emptied, and one column of numbers after another vanished over the horizon. They vanished from my sight at the point where the plain and infinity seemed to touch one another. My attention remained fixed on the horizon. I thought I could cover that distance in just a few steps, but then it suddenly seemed as though it was light years away. As my gaze wandered back and forth between myself and that far off horizon, I saw a tiny dot detach itself from the line where plain and sky met and slowly grow into a circle as it drew nearer. I felt it clearly, but couldn't see it with my eyes. It seemed to be a vibration rather than a solid object. As it drew closer and grew ever larger I suddenly saw a gigantic circular blossom in the place where I had previously felt the vibrations. Five transparent petals reflected a marvelous spectrum of color. More and more objects filled the vibrational field of this invisible circle: ice crystals formed radiant hexagonal stars, strange geometrical figures such as intertwining triangles and squares, a sphere half black, half white, harmoniously sharing a common center and unfolding before me a pattern such as I had never seen. Every element in the circle vibrated with its own rhythm, and yet all were so wonderfully synchronized. I was so moved I began running toward this vision... Then I woke up, and found myself lying on the floor next to my tabla.

When I once again entered the little room where Mohamed Ahmed Khan lived, I found him sitting, playing his tabla. I bowed to him and was received by a long, profound look between us. He seemed to have already noticed that I had experienced something far-reaching. After I had told him, as best I could, about my experiences, he asked me to play that simple flow of sixteen beats which he had taught me at the beginning of our time together—the one I had been playing the night of my dream.

DHA	DHIN	DHIN	DHA
DHA	DHIN	DHIN	DHA
DHA	TIN	TIN	TA
TETE	DHIN	DHIN	DHA...

When Mohamed Khan sensed that my playing had begun to flow, he started to play all the sixteen-beat compositions I had learned. I felt joyous as his playing joined with my simple rhythmic cycle. Then, Mohamed Khan changed to the *twelve-beat* cycle in that composition, which had so confused me on the previous occasion. My body reacted immediately, and I observed how my rhythmic flow began to falter. My hands found it difficult to continue playing, and I was on the verge of stopping when I suddenly realized that I could hear *both* rhythmic cycles simultaneously. A new power within carried me on simply and effortlessly. I felt his twelve and my sixteen beats meet in a *joint cycle*. At the same time my linear concept about rhythm vanished and a new image appeared inside myself: the two lines, different in length and impossible to combine finally met in the joint cycle of 12 and 16.

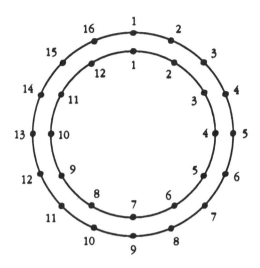

The Joint Cycle

The joint cycle is also a form of synchronization. Two pulsations meet in one place, then go separate ways before they meet again. The crucial difference between this kind of synchronization and the ones you have already experienced, is that here the intervals in both pulsations are always different. We could say that both pulsations have profoundly different character. The magic of the joint cycle occurs when these different characters meet in a clear relationship.

There are many possible ratios for joint cycles: 2:3, 3:4, 3:5, 3:8, 4:3, 4:7, and so on are joint cycles that serve as foundations for the rhythms of many cultures. The ratio 3:4, for example, means: while one pulsation vibrates three times, the other pulsation vibrates 4 times. Of course, both pulsations can be filled with rhythmic figures. The rhythmic phenomenon that results from this form of synchronization is called *polyrhythm*. Let's begin by experiencing the simplest one.

TA KI and GA MA LA are different rhythmic worlds. The transition from one to the other—both in the realm of units and cycles, and in the subdivision of intervals—brings about a different bodily feeling. So far, TA KI and GA MA LA have been felt and heard *one after the other*. In the following exercise, however, we will feel how both affect your body *simultaneously*.

7   The walking pulsation provides the rhythmic basis for this exercise to be done with Example 7. It will enable you to feel two different pulsations in your body *simultaneously*.

First, get in step with the pulsation of the *surdo*. Notice that the syllable GA coincides with each step. Now start clapping with the *moktak* on every other step.

Allow yourself to feel a new rhythmic energy arise when an additional clap is added on every other LA.

The *moktak* (and your clap) then begins playing every other MA, and thereby creates a different feeling in your walking. You now feel a *joint cycle,* based on two different pulsations which meet each time a clap and a step coincide.

The vocal rhythms you hear in the example allow you to alternately feel one pulsation more clearly than the other.

At this point, I remind you that each exercise builds slowly from a simple beginning. You can stay with the basic elements and still learn other aspects simply by listening. Do only as much as your body can playfully accept. If you feel that you're straining while clapping, then stop clapping and concentrate on your steps. If you have no difficulty with clapping, then bring that out by saying a GO with each clap to emphasize the three-beat cycle.

You can attempt the same thing with your steps. Then use the vocal GO, alternately, on the steps and claps. At the end of this example, notice the effect the drums have on you.

In the space between these points of contact, however, the two pulsations go their separate ways. You take two steps while clapping three times and thus create a different feel in the hands and feet. The most important point here is that the interval between each clap and between each step differs in quality. This quality is responsible for the creation of two different bodily feelings.

The following illustration shows the pulsation ratio of 2:3

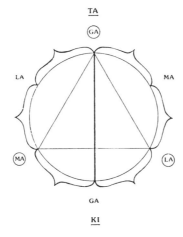

We have already used the circle to represent a variety of rhythmic phenomena. Now we discover that the circle also allows us to see the relationship of the two different rhythmic motions of the joint cycle. Both your body and the cycle are entities which represent wholeness and both are capable of uniting several different rhythmic motions.

The two pulsations in a joint cycle can be perceived in *three different ways*. The *first* is to perceive both pulsations simultaneously each with the same intensity. You can test your ability to perceive several events at the same time with the following experiment: draw a circle in the air with your *left* hand and allow yourself time to clearly feel both the movement and the size of the circle. Keep drawing the circle while you try to draw a triangle with your *right* hand, and observe your inner experience. Of course you can easily draw either shape by itself, but you will probably have some initial difficulty in doing both movements simultaneously. Remind yourself that it's only a game for developing simultaneous perception. You may at some time have consciously experienced the simultaneity of a bird singing nearby, a brook babbling at your feet, and someone talking to you. Each of these three acoustic levels has different sounds, different patterns, and probably also differences in volume. We often perceive all three levels as a single background of noise. At some moments, however, we may perceive all three levels as if we were simultaneously in three different worlds.

The *second way* is by hearing one of the two as the dominant pulsation. We then hear the second pulsation from the "perspective" of the dominant one. This is always the case when we structure one pulsation with rhythmic figures so that it becomes paramount and is thus perceived as the foundation.

The *third way* entails hearing both pulsations as one linear rhythmic figure. Two different rhythmic energies then merge into a one-dimensional pattern.

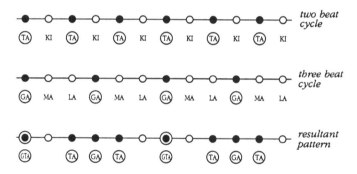

This pattern of one dimension results when two pulsations of different quality combine and is therefore called a *resultant pattern*. Many possibilities are available to capture and challenge the listener's imagination. The multi-dimensional rhythmic movement in a joint context fascinates the ear and stimulates levels of multi-dimensionality that are alive within the listener.

Additive and Divisive Cycles

Let us look again at the two ways in which cycles are created. If a long and a short influence a pulsation, then *unequal units* are added together to form a cycle. Extension of that principle produces the *additive cycle*. If, on the other hand, two pulsations interact, they generate *equal units* which, as we know, are also *cycles.* The pulses which the cycle encompasses *divide* the cycle into equal parts. The superimposition of pulsations creates the multiplicity of *divisive cycles.* We have already learned that in a two-beat cycle a basic pulsation vibrates with one that is half as fast.

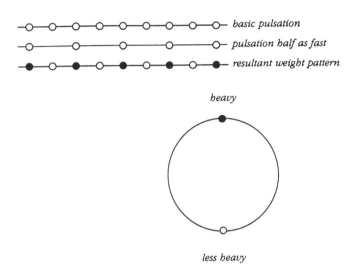

In the divisive three-beat cycle, the weight pattern results from the superimposition of a basic pulsation and one that is three times slower. You have experienced this three-beat cycle through the GA MA LA step.

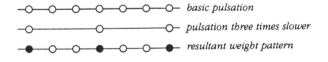

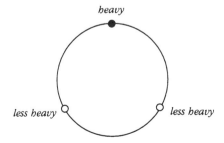

In the four-beat cycle, we encounter a new phenomenon. Whenever a basic pulsation meets a pulsation vibrating four times slower, an additional resonant pulsation is created which divides the four-beat cycle into *two* equal parts. This resonant pulsation vibrates half as fast as the basic pulsation. The weight pattern of the four-beat cycle results from the sum of all three pulsations. The third pulse thus becomes somewhat heavier, creating a fresh nuance in the weight pattern.

This stress on the third beat also divides the cycle into equal parts. A divisive cycle is therefore always symmetrical. You can experience the weight pattern of a four-beat cycle by practicing the TA KE TI NA step as presented in Chapter 6.

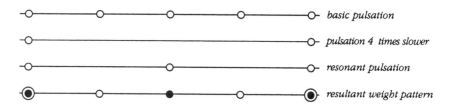

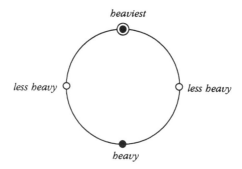

Looking deeper into the world of *divisive* cycles, we see that the five-beat cycle lacks a resonant pulsation. Five is a prime number and thus only divisible by itself. This cycle's weight pattern reveals that the first pulse is the heaviest while all others are equal in weight.

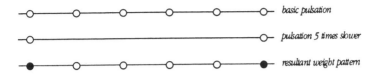

In the six-beat cycle, on the other hand, we find two different resonant pulsations, which create two different weight patterns.

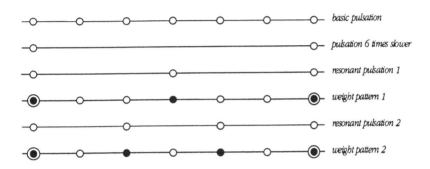

Depending on its structure, each cycle will have a different impact. It is therefore apparent that the laws of vibration which govern the production of overtones and other acoustic phenomena of vibrating strings, bars, air columns, etc., have a counterpart in the realm of the divisive cycle.

Cycles in which *units of different size* follow one another are called *additive cycles*. We sense their asymmetry from the weight pattern. The simplest succession of a long and a short establishes a three-beat cycle which appears in two different forms:

Voice   TA KI TIT TA KI TIT TA KI TIT   *or*

Voice   TIT TA KI TIT TA KI TIT TA KI

There are two ways in which additive cycles can expand beyond this basic form. On the one hand, both the long and short elements can include additional beats. On the other, we can combine as many long and short elements as we like by simple expansion. The additive five-beat cycle (2+3) may be expanded into a nine-beat cycle (2 + 3 + 4) by the addition of a four-beat unit.

Clap	○ · ○ · · ○ · ○ · ·
Voice	TA KI GA MA LA TA KI GA MA LA

Clap	○ · ○ · · ○ · · · ○
Voice	TA KI GA MA LA TA KE TI NA TA

8   In Example 8, you can hear the joint cycle of an additive 9 beat cycle and a divisive 6 beat cycle. The additive structure

TA KI GA MA LA TA KE TI NA

can first be heard on the *rantang*, a bamboo instrument from East Bali. Then other additive forms are gradually included before the divisive six beat cycle starts to sound. Listen without strain, and each time you might hear a new level of rhythmic movement.

The Inaudible Matrix of Rhythm

The silent pulse is the inaudible power behind every pulsation. The existence of an audible and an inaudible part as two aspects of one and the same rhythmic phenomenon is not, however, restricted to pulsation. Every rhythmic manifestation has an inaudible part in which its impact is anchored. The inaudible part of a cycle is its *weight pattern*. The audible part can be any creation that is meaningful in the context of the weight pattern. Both parts together produce the cycle.

It may be that both parts are identical. That is the case when a musician plays only the exact structure of a weight pattern. However, a musician will, most of the time, deviate from playing the weight pattern and go his own way within the framework of the cycle. The weight pattern nevertheless remains the source of orientation for both musician and listener. A well developed rhythmic awareness enables a musician to play outside of the weight pattern without losing his orientation.

The cycle's weight pattern flows on its own through such a musician, carrying him and creating an open space—a space for creative play. As the inaudible part of a cycle, this pattern exists in a universal archetypal realm. The audible shaping of the cycle, on the other hand, exists in the realm of uniqueness and individuality. In rhythm, both sides unite and thereby allow the individual to make contact with the world of archetypes.

If we become overly involved in the creation of rhythms, we may lose touch with the weight pattern. When this flow is lost, we inevitably fall out of rhythm. Then all structuring becomes meaningless and the importance of the primal rhythmic ground becomes apparent. The experience of falling out of rhythm shows us that rhythm cannot be willfully imposed.

This experience also leads us back to the qualities of voluntary and involuntary movements. The ultimate goal in rhythm is to be able to connect with both simultaneously. If we are only in the mode of involuntary movement, we are unable to create, and if we are only connected with the voluntary side, we will soon lose our connection to the inaudible matrix of rhythm. All creations will then become meaningless. The simultaneity of these two worlds seems to be the secret of rhythmic stability, which develops naturally as we lose our fear of falling out. I have worked with many people who have a deep fear of making mistakes and falling out of rhythm. They seem to believe that rhythmic stability increases by avoiding mistakes or falling out. From my teaching experience, the opposite is the case. It is a lesson which human physiology teaches us: it is not the final goal in any living system to reach a point of ultimate stability, but rather to fluctuate between a state of stability and instability. This fluctuation seems to renew the power of a rhythmic system.

Rhythmic power and stability develop when we allow ourselves to fall out of rhythm and come back into it while others continue to play a supportive rhythmic foundation. With the opportunity to return to the flow, we are able to confront our fear about losing rhythm; in this way, we learn to let ourselves be carried by the power of rhythm.

5

ARCHETYPES OF RHYTHM

The rich diversity of musical styles throughout the world is the product of both cultural and individual uniqueness. These vast differences are nonetheless all rooted in a common basis as archetypes which live in every human being from the moment of conception to the final breath. We access the power of an archetype only by an internal recognition which then allows us to sense it in the outer world. Musical archetypes exist in the world of sound and rhythm and both of these are governed by the natural laws of vibration which unfold an abundance of melodic and rhythmic forms. In the rhythmic sphere, the basic underlying archetypes are the phenomena of *cycles* and *subdividing pulsations* in the intervals. We experience the cycle in many ways: the recurring week which combines seven daily "pulses"; the flowing of the breath, which combines inhalation, exhalation and rest; a flower presenting a visible and tangible cycle in its petals. Subdividing pulsations create many rhythmic forms that we constantly encounter in our daily lives. For example, the mobility and self dividing tendency of intervals can be found in the behavior of vibrating strings and air columns.

Pulsation, cycle and *rhythmic movement within the interval* are the three primary realms in rhythm which all cultures, independently of one another, have discovered and used in their music in similar ways. This inevitability results from the laws of vibration and natural rhythms which are experienced by all humans. From these three primary elements, each culture has developed its own diversity of rhythms. As we go deeper into the possibilities of rhythmic unfolding, it leads us into the realm of rhythmic *figures* and the specific sound with which they are played on instruments in individual cultures. The seemingly endless possibilities for creating rhythmic figures produces a vast array, each with its own individual character. The creation of rhythmic figures by individuals lends the music of each culture its unique character.

Nonetheless, even the world of rhythmic figures contains archetypal correlations. I have encountered identical figures in Brazil and Korea—two cultures that presumably have not had cultural or musical exchange. But because the instruments employed produce such vastly different tonal colors, we may not immediately perceive the figure as one and the same rhythm. Such figures indicate to what extent the archetype extends into the "individual sphere" which refers to *individual consciousness* whereas archetypes are the product of *collective consciousness.*

In the realm of rhythm, pulsation and various pulsation ratios are the fundamental archetypes which, in the realm of vibration, are manifested as sound. Both are subject to the same laws which, as rhythmic pulsation, most frequently combine in ratios of 1:1, 1:2, 1:3, 2:3, 3:4, or 4:5. This is also true of any vibrating media (strings, wood, metal, etc.) and even in some species of fish whose fin movements are primarily coordinated in whole-number ratios.* The lower a ratio is, the more stable the relationship between two pulsations, whereas higher ratios bring about greater tension. This is true of both rhythmic and vibrational ratios. The frequency ratio of 15:16 produces a pitch interval of a minor second which creates much more tension than, for example, the fifth, with its frequency ratio of 2:3.

Remember that audible pulsations in the slow realm are the foundation for musical rhythms. A fast pulsation on the other hand, produces a tone. As two rhythmic pulsations can be related in a certain ratio (e.g. 2:3) so can two tones. The relationship between two pulsations of different quality is called *joint cycle* and the relationship between different tones is called *pitch interval,* or simply *interval.* The mathematical laws governing the creation of intervals were formulated by Pythagoras who used an instrument called a *monochord.* This ancient instrument is simply a string stretched over a wooden sound box with a moveable bridge to divide the string into two vibrating parts. The fundamental tone of the monochord's undivided string depends on its length, tension and the material from which it is made. The modern monochord illustrated here has several strings which are all tuned to the same fundamental note. This allows easy comparison of an undivided string with a divided one by enabling us to hear several intervals at once.

*E. VanHolst. The Relative Coordination as Phenomenon.

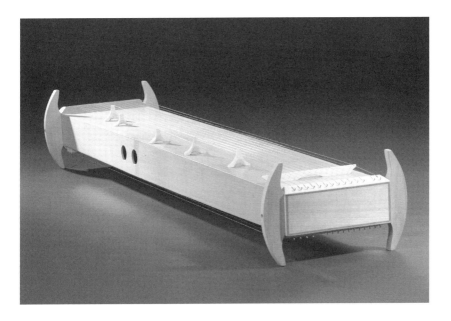

Monochord

The monochord shows us an additional relationship: the frequency ratio of an interval corresponds exactly to the string length (ratio) needed to produce the interval. For example, if the bridge is moved to the exact middle of the string, the two equal halves will vibrate precisely twice as fast as the undivided string. The ratio of the whole to the half is 1:2 in terms of both length and vibration. This ratio is called the *interval of an octave* and it corresponds to the rhythmic ratio known as "double-time." In the double-time relationship, one of the pulsations vibrates twice as fast, just as when two strings are tuned in an octave, one vibrates twice as fast. This correlation applies, of course, to the pulsation ratio of 2:3, presented as a bodily experience in Chapter 4, as "The Joint Cycle." If one of two strings, both tuned to the same tone, is divided at a point two-thirds of its length, then the resulting interval will be a perfect fifth when both sound together.

Both length and frequency ratio is 2:3. The series of frequency ratios proceeds as follows:

3:4	produces the perfect fourth
3:5	produces the major sixth
4:5	produces the major third

These ratios are the basis of many world rhythms. Each ratio produces its own unique rhythmic character as it does in the realm of sonic vibration with its intervallic ratios.

9   In Example 9, you hear the sound of various intervals played on a monochord. First, the octave with a ratio of 1:2, the fifth at a ratio of 2:3, and the fourth at 3:4. Notice how the sound of these intervals becomes more charged with tension as the numerical ratios increase:

5:9	produces the minor seventh
8:9	produces the major second
8:15	produces the major seventh
15:16	produces the minor second

In the realm of musical rhythm, a pulsation behaves just as it does in the realm of the intervals. So few points of joint contact exist between the two rhythmic pulsations in a ratio of 15:16 that they are not feasible as a basis for musical rhythm.

Sound Bowl

These vibrational laws affect not only the vibrating string of a monochord, but any vibrating material as well. We, ourselves, can embody these laws. With a little practice, anyone can sing a note and at the same time allow several other notes to sound. These notes are *overtones* and the same ones occur regardless of the particular voice. The phenomenon of *overtones* (harmonics) was presented in Chapter 4, "The Sub-Division of the Interval." Like a prism splitting up apparently colorless light into a visible spectrum of colors, the human voice has the capacity to develop a sung note into a spectrum of different frequency ratios. This *overtone singing* exists in many cultures and is a direct way of entering into a bodily relationship with the inexhaustible power of vibrational archetypes. In Example 10, you will hear sounds 10 which demonstrate that laws governing overtones apply to all vibrating phenomena: the voice, a simple plastic pipe swung rapidly around, sound bowls controlled by adjusting the mouth cavity and various waterphones.

Familiarity with the ratios produced on the monochord leads to a recognition that these proportions also apply to the overtone series. In every vibrating string, the main vibration (fundamental) is accompanied by several superimposed vibrations, or *partials,* which divide the string into two, three, four, and more, equal parts.

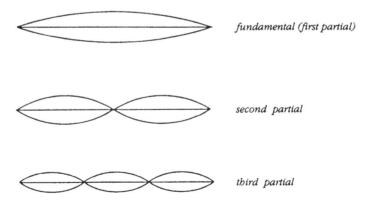

fundamental (first partial)

second partial

third partial

These superimposed vibrations are much weaker than the fundamental and therefore quieter. They are so quiet that they are not normally heard except as tonal coloring of the fundamental. In overtone singing, however, these partials sound out quite independently. Each additional partial divides the string into a higher ratio. Here again, the law stating that low-number ratios are more stable and occur more frequently applies.

Overtone Series

The first overtone to occur is:

the octave	(1:2)
then the fifth	(2:3)
followed by another octave	(1:4)
and a major third	(4:5)

Only later come the more charged intervals such as:

the minor seventh	(5:9)
the major second	(8:9)
and the major seventh	(8:15)

Pulsation, beat and offbeat, subdivisions of two and three, as well as double and triple units, are anchored in a deep human knowledge; they are part of our ancestral memories. In music, we acknowledge the equal value of beat and offbeat. This can be reflected in our daily life by our acceptance of differing points of view. Because of these rhythmic archetypes all human beings connect rhythmic phenomena with the same or similar feelings and experiences.

The power of a pulsation connects everyone with the feeling of being carried by rhythm. We first encounter this in the sound-world of the womb where the acoustic environment is shaped by two primal sound sources: the pulsating of the mother's heart and her voice which is heard as a high-frequency rustling and hissing. As heard in the recordings made by Alfred Tomatis,* these sounds are reminiscent of a rattle, especially when the flow of the mother's speech is rhythmic.

When we physically sense the supportive power of a pulsation, it creates within us the psychological qualities associated with being carried: a feeling of effortlessness and safety, and the inner knowledge that life has the power to carry us, if we allow it.

---

*A. Tomatis, The Conscious Ear, Station Hill Press, 1991

Because we can access the feeling of being carried with the help of a musical pulsation, it is a powerful healing tool. The psychological qualities of a pulsation are subconscious messages in daily life as well as in music. When musicians allow themselves to be carried by the silent pulse, the listener will connect consciously or unconsciously to the feeling of being carried. The music touches the body through its supportive foundation be it a classical piano sonata or the rhythms of an African drummer. Herein lies the power of rhythm to heal us when we seem to have lost that supportive feeling.

Another message that rhythm has for us, is, that conventional time is simply a mental construct. Rhythm enables us to connect with the tremendous power of timelessness. Of course, in each profound meditation you will connect more or less deeply with this state of mind. Rhythm, however, connects us very easily with timelessness and stillness of the mind as it clearly distinguishes between dreaming and true emptiness since dreams and thoughts will immediately throw us out of rhythm.

In our own way, we have all had extraordinary experiences of time. There have been several such moments for me, and in one of them I see myself sitting in a meadow by a small stream. It is summer and I hear the murmuring, babbling and splashing of the water uniting with the surrounding sounds. The sun dazzles in the ripples and gradually begins to dance before my eyes in a thousand different forms; a small cloud passes in front of the sun and the dance ceases. Now my gaze penetrates to the streambed. The countless shapes of the stones attracts me and the tranquility of their existence touches me...

Everyone knows, consciously or unconsciously, this "other sense of time." Some describe it as a wave standing still while all around it the water flows on. Others simply refer to this state as the experience of the present moment. Through bodily experience of the cycle, we release ourselves from linear time and approach a state of the perpetual present moment. The cycle has the power to alter our sense of time as we listen to music. It brings us into the here and now. Because pulsation, cycle and subdividing-pulsation exist as archetypes in all of us, many musicians of different cultures are able to combine their talents in the creation of a new world music. Rhythm is thus a world language that connects all human beings.

6

THE HUMAN BODY
AS MUSICAL INSTRUMENT

After studying classical piano, my learning path led to countries like India, Thailand, Indonesia, Korea, Japan, Cuba, Puerto Rico and Brazil. There I heard music that I initially found remote and I attempted to pick up rhythms that seemed incomprehensible. Challenged with many different kinds of behavior, food, and emotions, I asked myself time and again: "What has all this got to do with me and why am I, a classically trained pianist, trying to learn all these rhythms that don't seem to have any common context? And even if I could master these drum rhythms, how would they fit into my life?" Thousands of questions surfaced every day. Nonethless, a strange but clear feeling that this deeply affecting experience would someday be valuable, allowed me to continue my pursuit without wavering.

During this time, I discovered that these new rhythms could most easily be played with my body. I embodied my basic pulsation in walking. With my voice, I created a supportive foundation of rhythmic words, or imitated the sound-sequences of rhythms and by clapping accents I generated rhythmic structures. Wherever I happened to be, I could use my body-instrument for learning, and I soon realized this discovery exerted a powerful influence on my daily life.

What I had initially viewed as merely an aid for practicing, was now leading me toward a wholly different way of experiencing rhythm. As the connection between rhythm and my life gradually became apparent, my footsteps and my life itself gained security. My doubts about whether I would become as good a drummer as my teacher gradually dispelled and I gained the inner space I needed to learn new rhythms. I found it easier to accept myself—what I could and could not do. The speaking of rhythms changed the flow of my speech, the sound of my voice and the phrasing of my sentences. My words gained a greater impact and I developed a new ability for rhythmic interplay in conversation.

I was totally preoccupied with these changes in my life and I systematically tried all the rhythms I knew on my body. As I explored the rhythmic possibilities of my body in greater depth, more levels opened up. Right and left gradually became rhythmically autonomous and as time went on, I found greater freedom in the interaction of the three levels: voice, hands and feet. When I felt my hands and feet carry out completely different rhythmic movements, it was like being freed from chains.

Before I found rhythm as my path, I attempted to learn music by studying the piano, but something seemed to inhibit the flow of my fingers and the music seldom sounded right to me. Later on, when I began learning different styles of drumming, my experience was quite different, and the study of several types of drums at once revealed a whole new quality of learning. It was no longer possible for me to hold on to technical details, so it became necessary to discover new ways of learning. I started to play and memorize rhythms with my body so that all I then had to do was transpose them to the drums. My piano playing also changed when I discovered that my technical problems had been simply a lack of rhythmic body consciousness. Once the primary rhythmic elements were understood by my body, even the most basic practice became more musical. I realized that the wonderful diversity of musical instruments was created from a single original instrument—the human body.

The Heartbeat—Primal Pulse of Music

Long before we see the light of this world, we live in the pulsating sound world of the womb. Our mother's heartbeat and voice are the first rhythmic impressions that shape our consciousness. In this rhythmic sound world, there arises the first communication between mother and child. In this time of our life, pulsation is a constant and profound experience. The mother's pulse, the pulsating rocking of her body and the sense of being carried create a totally integrated environment. The pulsating of music reminds us of this primal experience. The heartbeat is an elemental rhythmic measure within ourselves which embodies a specific tempo that relates to all other pulsations and rhythms we play. It may become faster, slower or synchronize itself with the pulsation of a musical rhythm, but it always returns to its own tempo. When we feel our pulse, we sense this primal rhythmic power. We ourselves are this power. We encounter ourselves in our pulse! As we get to know the rhythm of our pulse, it becomes our companion in everyday life and we develop a relationship to our primal rhythmic ground.

The pulsing of the heart is produced by the alternating contraction and relaxation of the heart muscle. The contraction is known as the *systole*, and the relaxation as the *diastole*. Two parts of our nervous system, known as the *sympathetic* and the *para-sympathetic* are in constant control of the rhythm of the heartbeat. One stimulates, the other inhibits. The heartbeat is thus embedded in the forces at work in our nervous system. But the origin of this rhythmic power remains an absolute mystery. Put an ear to someone's chest and you will hear the heartbeat rhythm:

Bpp   Bmm   •   Bpp   Bmm   •   Bpp   Bmm

This "melody" divides the intervals between the pulses into three sub-dividing pulses. When the body moves more actively, the "melody" changes, and we hear intervals divided into two:

Bpp   Bmm   Bpp   Bmm   Bpp   Bmm   Bpp   Bmm

The heartbeat is a complicated rhythmic event, but we can experience it as a simple, supportive pulsation anywhere within the body where the pulse can be felt. We *hear* music with our body and *play* music with our body. The body and its rhythms play a central role in music. This is why we find a knowledge of the inner pulse in the music of all cultures. There are drums which directly imitate the melody of the heartbeat. The drumming of Native American shamans involves a direct musical transposition of the heartbeat and so, too, do certain rhythms played on the Korean *buk* and the Japanese *taiko*. The heartbeat also forms the rhythmic foundation for complex Indian rhythms. The pulse tempo is the measure for the slowest basic speed in Indian music, known as *vilambit laya*. Although this music uses many subtle tempo gradations, the Indian musician identifies three tempo ranges: *vilambit* (slow), *madhya* (moderate), *drut* (fast). *Madhya* is twice as fast as the pulse and *drut* four times as fast. The music of Africa, Latin America and Asia is full of instances where a link with the pulse rate is clearly perceptible. However, this knowledge also exists in Western music. The *Tactus integer valor* was the basis of European music from the mid-15th century until the end of the 16th century. It is the underlying pulse in Bach's music, and, at around 60 beats a minute, corresponds to a slow heartbeat.

Drum rhythms act on the human heartbeat. This is an essential power in the healing rituals of all cultures. The body rhythms of all participants change in accordance with the impact of the music played. Every healing rhythm is, like our pulse, multi-dimensional and this quality enables pulse and drum to touch one another. By multi-dimensionality, I mean a uniting of several rhythmic energies, just as the pulse has within itself possibilities of both double and triple time. Another important characteristic of a healing rhythm is its flexibility which allows subtle tempo variations—a phenomenon which strengthens the elasticity of our own pulse. The degree to which a natural pulsation fluctuates poses an interesting challenge for a musician: what does exactitude of playing mean from this perspective and how does it unite with a vital flexibility?

We all bear the measure of living pulsation within ourselves. When we are developing our rhythmic abilities, the precision of our playing is the result of a combination of motoric movement and listening. By listening, I mean attention directed both outward and inward. Each of these three abilities (motoric movement, outward listening, inward listening) can be focused by itself. But when all three come together, the outcome is a great degree of rhythmic stability and exactitude in conjunction with perceptible flexibility. Body movements and the hearing of sound both affect the same fluid in the ear. Therefore listening and bodily movement meet in the ear.*

Pulsations found in nature are not perfectly regular—they fluctuate. As things are in the outer world so are they within. By finding ways of strengthening the flexibility of our pulse, we gain vitality.

*A. Tomatis. *The Conscious Ear:* "Medical Scientists have long known that all bodily movements affect the vestibular fluid (the fluid of the organ of equilibrium), whereas acoustic rhythms mobilize the same fluid in the realm of the utriculus, semicircular canals and sacculus. That is why these elements of the vestibular apparatus are capable of reproducing integrated movements or storing them in the memory."

Breathing—Bodily Knowledge of Flow

Our life in this world begins with the first breath. This, and the cutting of the umbilical cord, are a step toward rhythmic autonomy. We are linked with the sensation of flow through the movement of the breath. Combining a body movement with an inhalation or exhalation generates a flowing movement, whereas a movement combined with the heartbeat gives rise to a pulsating movement. The pulse cannot ordinarily be directly and deliberately influenced, but with our breathing we can either inhale and exhale voluntarily or we can simply allow breathing to happen in its normal, involuntary manner. In breathing, we again encounter the co-existence of letting be and taking action—the two states whose interaction is an essential part of rhythm and music.

The flowing of the breath links the inside of our body with the outside. Through breathing, we are united with the "air body" of the earth. We inhale huge amounts of air—3,026 gallons of air flow through our body every 24 hours as we engage in an intensive exchange with our environment. There are places where we really can smell the energy in the air. In the mountains or at the ocean, the air is highly charged with energy—which in India is known as *prana*. With air rich in *prana,* we tend to eat less.

Taking in oxygen is only one function of breathing. Its real vital force lies in the untiring rhythmic movement. You experienced the phases of breathing in the first elementary rhythmic experiences offered in this book. The simplest case is merely an alternation of inhalation and exhalation. Your breathing flows on its own when you link the flowing of air into your body with the feeling of "letting in" and flowing out with a "letting go." In between there are two points of transition which play an important part in the rhythm of breathing. They have the ability to expand. When we are in a state of rest, there is a brief moment when breathing comes to a standstill after letting go. This moment has the quality of "letting be." Breathing out has come to an end and breathing in hasn't begun. It's a moment of stillness. It is that very moment which begins to expand as though by itself when we detach ourselves from activity and enter deeper levels of our consciousness as in sleep or meditation. As we allow ourselves to go deeper, this letting be extends itself to a period of time equal to each of the other two phases. We then breath in a triple cycle:

Inhalation phase — Exhalation phase — Stillness phase

However, when we are active, this space becomes ever shorter until it is finally just a point of transition. A *dual cycle* then arises in the alternation of inhalation and exhalation. After a fast run, we clearly experience this dual cycle in breathing. You can best hear and see triple-time when observing someone in a deep sleep. In the rhythm of breathing, dual time is associated with an extroverted attitude while triple time is a bodily expression of introversion. The point of transition after breathing in is potentially the fourth phase. There, the moment when breathing stops doesn't happen of its own accord. If we want to extend this point of transition, we must voluntarily retain the air that has streamed into us. This can happen effortlessly with practice. Nevertheless, we must do something deliberately, or else the air simply carries on flowing. Therefore, I call the point of transition after inhalation the *active* pole, and the point after exhalation the *passive* pole.

Inhalation and exhalation are like two energy fields that discharge at the moment of reversal. These are the moments when *prana* starts to flow. When these phases establish a rhythmic relationship, there begins a perceptible but silent music within our inner rhythms. The pulsating movement of the heartbeat then enters into relationship with the flowing of the breath. The relationship depends on the individual pulse rate. A simple relationship comes into being when the inhalation extends over three pulse-beats and the exhalation together with the pause in breathing stretches over six pulse beats. The Indian tradition of Pranayama has uncovered many such energy charged relationships between the flow of our breath and the rhythm of our pulse. Initially, such relations between our vital rhythms unfold as duple and triple cycles and then combine as complex cycles.

When playing an instrument, breathing provides very valuable feedback about the flow of the music. As we force the movement or lose the pulsation, breathing becomes constrained and fast. If you play a drum, try to make the flow of your breath audible by humming a sound as you play. What changes in your drumming? Can you hear the rhythm of your breath and the sound of your drums at the same time? If you try this for a while, your playing will become more clear and your rhythmic awareness will deepen.

The Voice—
A Direct Expression of Rhythmic Impulse

The breath and the voice form an indivisible entity. Through the voice, breathing becomes audible and through breathing, the voice resonates. The larynx and the vocal chords lie in the air stream of the breath and produce the tones which we form by way of a complex interaction of larynx muscles, oral cavity, tongue and lips. Various resonance areas in the head, chest, and stomach also participate in this vibration depending on which sound is involved. Feelings and sensations exert a direct impact on these delicate muscles. They open or close resonance areas thus becoming directly audible in the sound of the voice. The voice is the audible expression of our present psychic state and emotional character. Here, too, the voice and breath act as an entity.

The sound of a strangulated voice is usually associated with shallow breathing. The sound of the voice, the resonance areas, and the state of the vocal muscles are intertwined. This means that, on the one hand, a feeling can color the sound of the voice in a particular way while on the other, a particular vocal sound can spark off a feeling. If we succeed in opening a resonance area, it can happen that the breath will deepen. Development of the voice and singing thus provide valuable assistance toward emotional growth.

Here we are especially concerned with the rhythmic voice. In rhythmic languages, which have developed all over the world, the voice leaves recitation and forms pulsating rhythms using a variety of sounds. Pulsation functions as support, therefore, a rhythmic language gives the voice a supportive rhythmic role. Something important happens here. We cannot bring about a state of being carried—not even in the case of the voice. So in speaking a rhythmic language we approach a state in which the voice sounds out independently of our will. We thereby arouse the pulsative power in our voice. I am referring to the very quiet voice which only awakens after prolonged inner listening. It is not always available—as the recitational voice is.

In recitative speech, we can express ourselves at will but the gentle supportive voice always starts within. You have already experienced rhythm as an inner voice. Even before it becomes audible, it can link up with the movements of your body. This endows the rhythmic movement with great security and breathes life into them. It may be that for you, this inner voice means listening rather than speaking. Both ways are equally valid since both inner listening and speaking are one and the same in the inner voice. When this pulsating inner voice starts to sound out, you will immediately feel its supportive lightness.

The voice makes possible a direct expression of rhythmic impulse. It also enables us to shape very different sounds into rhythms. After considerable practice, it becomes possible at many speeds. All of these capabilities make the voice a full-fledged percussion instrument.

The Rhythmic Formative Levels of the Body

The three levels our body offers for creating a variety of sounds and audible rhythms are:

> Voice
> Hands
> Feet

The entire world of rhythm can be experienced with the body through the interaction of these levels. Each one serves a primary rhythmic function: the feet carry us, the hands shape, and the voice connects our clapping and walking. The voice in particular has two equally strong capabilities; to structure and to create a supportive ground. By developing a rhythmic body consciousness, we can implement any rhythmic form at any level of the body. Pulsation can become audible through the voice, clapping or walking. The same applies to the combining of pulses: cycles and units come into existence through the speaking of rhythm words or the singing of a melody. Various basic steps make possible a whole-body experience of a cycle. Different clapping sounds can also combine several pulses within a single pulsation.

Each bodily level unfolds its own particular strength through its primary rhythmic function: the feet make contact with the ground and discover the state of being carried; the hands in creating and structuring rhythmic figures; and the voice in rhythmically linking the two other levels, by a quiet pulsating speech.

The rhythmic path of TA KE TI NA starts with the voice. You can hear the pulsation of the inner voice within yourself even before it becomes externally audible. When your voice starts to sound out, a rhythmic movement which arose inside yourself can be heard outside. The vocal rhythms can be combined in a variety of ways with the movements of hands and feet. The most elementary combination is created when the vocal pulsation coincides with a step or clap. The voice then connects with the bodily movement. If a vocal pulsation joins with the pulsation of walking, you may feel that the vocal pulses flow to the floor with every step, sending energy roots into the ground.

The Steps—Experiencing Cycles in the Body

Our personal rhythm and our character are expressed in the way we walk. We all experience the pulsation of walking in precisely the same way: through the alternation of left and right. But what an amazing diversity is found in the way people move! Spend a little time in a busy pedestrian zone, and you will discover the great range of characteristics revealed by people as they walk: flexibility and rigidity, rushing and calmly flowing, jerkiness and regularity and much more. You will see innumerable nuances and combinations of characteristics which have formed in the course of each life. Walking is not only a rhythmic form of expression but can also be a rhythm exercise of daily life. As we stroll, every step shows us how flexible our body is and how we make contact with the ground.

These sensations of flexibility and contact become more meaningful when we alter their flow by walking in place instead of moving forward. Walking in place makes it easier for us to see if and where we are blocking the flow of our steps. This pulsating movement is the basis for the various TA KE TI NA steps. Several pulses are combined in each step and for each cycle there is a specific sequence of steps. The following sections present the three most important basic steps.

The TA KI Step

Begin the TA KI step by walking to a steady pulsation. Gradually let the forward movement of your steps become smaller and smaller until you are walking in place. If you find yourself swaying from side to side, let that movement decrease until your head and upper body are as still as possible. Now, with every step, you can sense the growing intensity of the movement toward the ground. The smaller the movements of your steps become, the more subtly you are able to feel the increasing contact with the earth. If you direct your attention to the interval between the steps, your movements will grow lighter. You may sense a slight side to side movement in your pelvis and if you accept it your movement will become more flowing. Now add your voice by joining your right foot with the syllable TA and your left foot with KI. With this TA KI step you embody a cycle of two pulses.

The GA MA LA Step

11

A three beat cycle can be experienced in the GA MA LA step. Use Example 11 for the following exercise which starts with the simple TA KI step.

Walk to the beat of the surdo—the right foot on TA and the left on KI and gradually begin to walk in place. Change your syllables from TA KI to GA MA LA when it occurs in the recording. Your foot movement remains the same and each step is accompanied by a syllable. Observe how GA first occurs with the right foot and next with the left. Direct your attention to GA and take a small step forward each time the GA occurs. Notice how the movement of your feet outline a triangle. Allow your movements to be carried by the sound of the instruments and follow the *moktak* with your clap. The clapping coincides with the step on GA which is the first beat of the three-beat cycle. By responding to my TIN GO vocalizations, you will gain a stronger sense of the three-beat cycle. It may also be that these vocal rhythms cause you to fall out of the stepping or clapping. This is a necessary process when learning to experience several rhythmic levels simultaneously. Allow chaos to happen so that your inner knowledge of rhythm can surface. When this happens, go back to the GA MA LA step as you hear it on the recording. When the clap moves to the syllable MA, the GA still remains the start of the three-beat cycle. You'll be able to feel that clearly when responding to the vocal rhythms. As the end of the example draws near, let your steps become ever smaller. Your body will then have "memorized" the weight pattern of the three-beat cycle.

The TA KE TI NA Step

Read through this entire section first, and then listen to the simple pulse 12 of TA KE TI NA on Example 12. Place the depiction of the TA KE TI NA basic step, found on the next double pages, on the floor and look at the illustration while you speak the syllables heard on Example 12.

The TA KE TI NA step is performed as follows:

(1) TA: Standing with feet comfortably apart, lift the right foot and return it to the same place.

(2) KE: Lift your right foot again and take a small side step to the right and shift your body weight onto it.

(3) TI: Lift your left foot and side step toward the right foot.

(4) NA: Lift the left foot again and side step to the left and once again shift your body weight.

(1) TA: Return right foot to starting position and continue steps 2 through 4 as above.

Give yourself enough time to match your steps to the syllables. When your voice and steps are together, close your eyes and feel this movement. Give yourself time to feel the shift of your weight as you move from step to step. Although you are moving from side to side, you may sense within yourself a circular movement beginning and ending with TA. You are now feeling the four-beat cycle, and, as in the previous examples, claps and vocal rhythms are gradually added. You can then feel the four-beat cycle more clearly and experience several rhythmic levels simultaneously. Try to answer the vocal rhythms you hear while maintaining your steps and clapping.

As the music fades, let your steps get smaller and smaller until you hardly sense any bodily movement. The movement of the cycle will, however, continue to flow within if you listen for it. Thus, the cycle of four beats manifests itself in the TA KE TI NA step.

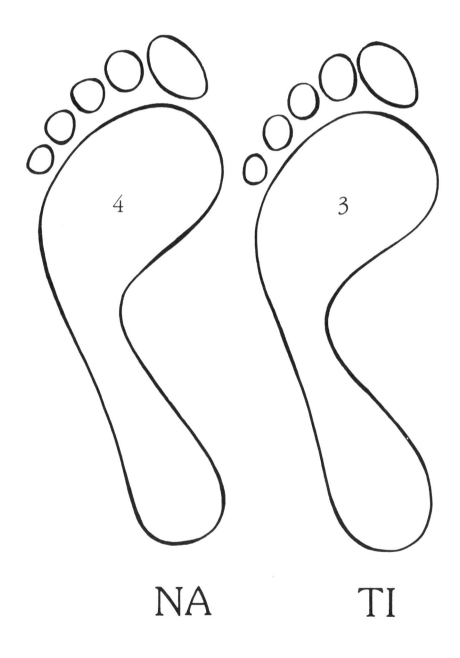

NA   TI

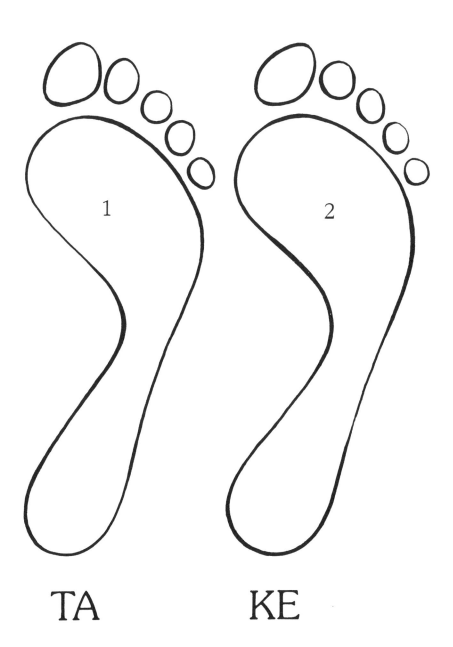

TA   KE

Three Combinations of Voice and Clapping

Voice Forms Foundation—Clapping Creates Rhythm

You can create rhythms by clapping over a supportive, pulsating voice. The supportive foundation in the voice will be brought into being if you repeatedly speak or sing one, two, or several sounds at regular intervals. A foundation thus arises in your voice. Clapping offers us a number of possibilities for creating sounds. Loud and soft clapping result from differences in intensity of movement. High clapping is produced by hitting the front of one hand with the back of the other. A deeper sounding clap is created by using cupped palms. You can extend these sound possibilities even further by snapping your fingers, rubbing your hands together and incorporating other parts of the body. These are some elementary possibilities for expression with the hands. Even though the arm and hand movements for drumming are more complex, the principle remains the same. You can thus experience the interaction of the supportive voice and the rhythmic structuring of your hands in clapping, drumming or in the playing of other musical instruments.

To begin, create a supportive foundation by vocalizing a regular pulsation of two tones or two syllables. Choose a moderate tempo for this singing or speaking and give yourself time to feel the vibration of your voice no matter how quiet it may be. When you feel your voice carrying you, begin clapping the simple rhythmic elements you already know (beat, off-beat, and double-time off-beat) and feel their effect on your vocal pulse.

When your vocalizing is secure, try to form different rhythmic combinations using these elements. You may gradually extend the vocal foundation to several tones or syllables by using GA MA LA, TA KE TI NA or other syllables which enable you to form a pulsation and a cycle.

If you can play a drum, try to play the rhythms you already know with the vocal pulsation of just one syllable. Speak a GO with each pulse of the rhythm that you're playing and notice how the voice sometimes wants to follow the accents set by your hands.

The interplay of vocal pulse and rhythmic clapping or drumming, develops our ability to feel several rhythmic levels simultaneously. We find that various cultures have a corresponding technique which allows the basic pulsation and cycle to become audible through a recurrent melody whose notes follow one another at regular intervals. This technique is used in India where a melody, known as the *lahara,* is often played as background for a drum solo. This melody remains unvaried throughout—just like your singing or speaking in the exercise—and provides orientation for the drum solo when playing in long rhythmic cycles.

Voice and Clapping Imitate One Another

We can imitate the rhythmic creations of the voice with clapping and reproduce the various sounds and rhythms of clapping with the voice. An audible supportive foundation is not created in this particular relationship. The rhythmic inventions and their imitations happen over a silent pulse. A special relationship thereby develops between voice and clapping which demands accurate listening in order to determine which rhythms and combinations of sounds should be repeated. The listening must, at the same time, constantly sense the silent pulse.

In basic imitation, the correspondences are simple: the response to a high and low clap is, of course, a high and low vocal sound. The clapping imitates the structure presented by the voice or vice versa. At first, it may happen that the silent pulse is no longer clearly perceptible during such shaping and imitation. It is then helpful to attempt creation and imitation to the pulsation of walking. Take, for instance, a high syllable TIN and a deeper GO as your vocal sounds. You can answer them with a high and low clap. These sounds are produced, as you know, by using the back of the hand or cupped palms. Initially, you need to practice a little in order to clearly differentiate the two clapping sounds. As soon as these different sounds can be produced easily, you can start structuring.

Begin with a pulsating walk. Take the time to sense the supportive power of your walking and then start to speak the two syllables to the pulsation of your walking. When you imitate these syllables by clapping, both the vocal sounds and the corresponding claps are beats within the pulsation of your walk. This is an easy way to begin since you only need concentrate on the imitation of sounds.

Voice and Clap	TIN	GO	high clap	low clap
Step				

When you feel sure of yourself, allow the vocal rhythms to become more complex. You will continue to feel the underlying pulse through the pulsation of walking. The creation and the imitation of a structure do not necessarily have to follow one another. When the voice creates while the clapping imitates, we have the experience of simultaneity. Movements on the two bodily levels then join to form a spontaneous simultaneity.

If you play a drum, try to experience this simultaneity by speaking the rhythms you play. Then reverse that by drumming the rhythms you speak. Simultaneity in both body levels creates a high degree of awareness in rhythmic structuring, and enables a drummer to develop a spontaneous expressiveness. The link between the voice and clapping is the foundation for the various "drum languages" found throughout the world. Just as you imitated the simple sounds of your clapping in this exercise, so can a drum language imitate the sound of a drum. Several of these drum languages are presented in the final section of this chapter.

Voice Creates Rhythm—Clapping Forms Foundation

Now the clapping takes the supportive role, allowing the voice to create freely. The foundation provided by your clapping can be a simple pulsation using sounds at a steady dynamic level. The alternation of different clapping sounds causes several pulses to be combined, thus creating units and cycles.

Start with the simplest thing—a regularly pulsating clap over which you can improvise by singing or vocalized rhythms. Then try clapping a succession of units of different length—for example:

Clap	◯ • • ◯ • ◯ • • ◯ •
Voice	GA MA LA TA KI GA MA LA TA KI

When your speech rhythm and clapping provide a supportive flow, let your voice gradually get quiet until finally only the clapping remains. Allow yourself time to continue the speech rhythm with your inner voice. When you feel ready, try to sing or speak structures to the flow of your clapping. Example 4 may help with this exercise since you will constantly hear the rhythmic basis of the five-beat cycle.

4

If you play a drum, create a simple and unvaried rhythm, corresponding to the simple basis of the clapping. As soon as your playing carries you, allow your voice the freedom to sing or speak rhythmically. Make sure that your drum rhythm remains steady and the rhythmic figure you choose to play does not change. At this point, I remind you once again to do only those exercises which are easy and fun. If you learn only one step, that's enough for a beginning. The more time you take, the deeper your feeling and hearing will become. Then, as the various levels of your awareness meet in a joint rhythm, your rhythmic consciousness will expand.

This relationship of the voice creating the rhythm, while the clapping forms the foundation, provides the basis for time keeping in Indian music and all related forms. In Example 13, you hear a drum solo by the Indian 13 master of the *pakhavaj*, Pandit Arjun Shejwal. The *pakhavaj* is the oldest North Indian drum and we will look at it in greater detail in the final chapter. The playing is accompanied by the clapping which is normally heard during any Indian drum solo. This is known as *"giving the tala"*—the clapping of the rhythmic foundation which employs three types of claps. The loudest clap signifies the first beat of a cycle. This is called *sam* in the Indian musical tradition, and its symbol is a cross (+). A soft clap signifies the start of a unit. These beats are called *tali* and they are designated by a number which refers to the units within a cycle in the sequence. An entire unit is left free by not clapping at all, using instead, a gesture, as you see in the third photo. This is known as *khali*, which can be translated as something akin to empty. Its symbol is the empty circle.

Sam *Tali* *Khali*

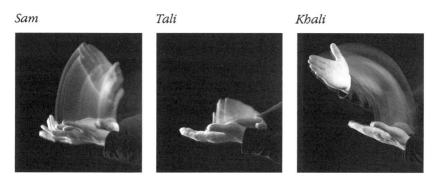

The rhythm you hear in Example 13 is called *chautal*. Six units, each of two beats, produce a cycle of 12 beats. The weight of the first pulse-beat in each unit varies so that these pulses combine as a longer cycle. *Chautal's* weight pattern:

TALA CHAUTALA

+		○		II		○		III		IV	
1	2	3	4	5	6	7	8	9	10	11	12
Dhā	dhā	dhin	tā	Tit	dhā	Dhin	tā	Tit	kata	Gadi	ghene

The Hidden Power of Speech

As young children, we experiment with the sounds of speech which we are just beginning to develop. At that time, we conduct intensive research, still unhindered by the intellect, into the sound and rhythmic body of words. The sound of our voice and our speaking develops by imitation.

The sound of our voice, the dynamics and articulation of our speech, are an essential component of what we want to communicate with our words. We reveal ourselves in the way we speak. The manner of our speaking and the associated movements are an expression of our inner selves just as the way we walk reveals much about our personality. This brings into being a second level of communication, which underlines or contradicts the meaning of our words.

However, the words themselves also have a sonic and rhythmic body which constitutes their essence. In the development of language, a word's meaning, sound, and rhythm were originally a unity. In that form, a word is an immediate reality. The more we concentrate on the logical coherence of words, the more their sonic and rhythmic nature vanishes into the background. It is easy to dispel the logical meaning of a word by repeating it again and again for a considerable time, setting it off against a pulsation. If you repeat a word many, many times in succession, you'll notice after a while that this word becomes strange, and loses its conventional meaning. However, you'll probably discover a deeper meaning deriving from the sound of the syllables and the rhythm. If you open yourself to the sound of the syllables, your voice will vibrate more intensely on its own and reach areas of your body which correspond to the spoken syllables. Over time this brings about a change of consciousness since the vocal vibrations act on our muscles and bones, on our entire nervous system, various components of our brain and numerous energy currents that flow through our body.

Such energy words have arisen in all cultures. In the Indian tradition they are called *mantras*. "Man" signifies consciousness, and "tra" means tool. A *mantra* is a tool for the development of consciousness. TA KI, GA MA LA, TA KE TI NA, etc. are *mantras* for the development of rhythmic consciousness. In their simplest form they help us experience *rhythmic quantities*. This applies to both the combination of pulses and also to the various sub-dividing pulsation. However, in these *mantras*, there dwells a power which only becomes apparent after they've been spoken for a long time. Through these rhythmic *mantras*, the conscious connects with the unconscious. The involvement of deeper levels of our consciousness enables rhythm to flow as though by itself. Our waking awareness is thus freed for creative shaping.

Rhythm Languages

In all cultures, we find a development of linguistic forms that are simply an expression of rhythm. Rhythmic languages related to drumming have developed alongside the many varieties of mantras. There are three different ways to relate speech and drum:

To Speak like a drum	involves using the voice to imitate drum sounds.
To Speak by way of a drum	entails playing a drum sound which corresponds to a word.
To Speak for a drum	by charging it with the rhythmic energy of a *mantra*.

You have already encountered the principle of speaking like a drum. The reciprocal imitation of clapping and speech can simply be extended to drum and voice. With the voice, we can also create differentiated sounds at a very rapid tempo. The voice, being well suited for imitating drum rhythms, has enabled drum language to develop in various cultures. Within a culture, a drum language is always linked with a specific drum. As a drum sounds, so too does the drum language sound.

In Indian music, drum languages are very highly developed. A drummer learns to play his instrument through these languages. The teacher makes clear to his pupil from the start that rhythms can only be played as fast as the performer is capable of speaking them. In India, the various drum languages correspond in every way to the drumming itself. On several occasions, I have heard an Indian drummer simply recite rhythms for hours with his drums sitting quietly in front of him. The syllables in Indian drum languages are called *bolas* and they are also used in Indian notation.

The most frequently used drum in North Indian music today is the *tabla* which consists of a bulbous bass drum called the *bayan* and a conical wooden drum known as a *dayan*. The basic beat on the *bayan* is GHE, and on the *dayan,* TA. If both sound together it is DHA. TA TE TE TA is therefore a sequence of beats without the bass drum; DHA TE TE DHA is a combination with the bass drum played on the first and last beats.

14   In Example 14, you hear a number of simple *bola* combinations which are first spoken and then played. The ties under the *bolas* indicate beats in the basic pulsation. Western notation indicates the duration of a note whereas, in many non-European cultures, everything refers to the underlying pulsation. World rhythms are thus usually written in terms of pulsation. Example 14 starts with the basic sounds of the tabla and simple combinations. They are played here relatively slowly so that you can speak the individual *bolas* and experience this drum language directly.

Tabla

TA

GHE

TA TIT TA —

DHA TIT DHA —

DHA — TE TE DHA — — —

DHI NA GHE NA DHA — — —

DHA TIT — DHA — DHA GHE NA

DHA GHE NA DHA — DHA GHE NA

DHE RE DHE RE DHE RE DHE RE

TE RE TE RE KE TE TA KA

DHA — TE TE GHE RE NA GHE

DHI — NA — GHE RE NA GHE

DHA TE TE DHA TE TE DHA DHA TE TE DHA GHE DHI NA KE NA

DHA TRE KE DHE TE DHA GHE NA DHA TI GHE NA TIN NA KE NA

DHA TIT DHA GHE NA DHA TEREKETE DHA TIT DHA GHE TIN NA KE NA

In the second part of Example 14, you hear the drum language of the *pakhavaj,* spoken by Pandit Arjun Shejwal. You will learn more about the *tabla* and *pakhavaj* in Chapter 8.

Other Asian rhythmic traditions also have a drum language. In Korean music, this language imitates the *tschanggo.* This drum was played more than four thousand years ago by the Tunguse people. The membranes at both ends are hit with two different drumsticks. The left-hand membrane is hit with the *gungultsche* (a wood mallet) and the right hand skin with the *joltsche* (a thin bamboo stick) which produces a variety of sounds.

Tschanggo

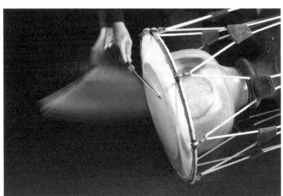

Tschepjon

Kungpjon

The Korean notation is also a pulsation notation with specific symbols for each drum sound. Here are the symbols for the most important *tschang-go* sounds:

⬡	KUNG	Open sound on the left hand skin, producing a resonant bass note.
❘	TOK	Open sound with the entire length of the right-hand drumstick, producing an accented light sound.
⦶	TONG	KUNG and TOK sounding together.
❘	KI TOK	A blow with the tip of the right-hand drumstick followed by TOK, creating a deeper, less stressed sound rapidly followed by a higher accented sound.
❘	KI KI TOK	Two blows with the tip of the right-hand drumstick followed by TOK produces a rapid succession of two deeper sounds followed by a higher accented sound.
❘	TORR	Bouncing action of the right-hand drumstick, giving rise to a rhythmically undefined sequence of the sound KI.
⧆	KU KUNG	Two open blows with the left-hand drumstick, producing a rapid succession of two resonant bass sounds with more stress on the second.

In Example 15, you again hear simple sound combinations, first spoken 15 and then played. By speaking these syllables, you will experience the difference of Indian and Korean drum languages.

From Africa's many drum languages, I present Ghana's *gamamla* music to show that a rhythmic language is not limited to the drum. *Gamamla* is played on a large number of tuned double bells called *gankogui*. In this case, TIN represents the longer sounding deeper bell, whereas the short percussive sound of the higher bell is imitated with a high, short GO. In Example 16, you will also experience the relationship of audible pulsation to silent pulse. 16 It starts with a simple pulsation played on a *moktak*. This simple pulsation is embellished by rhythmic figures on the *gankoguis*. Feel the *moktak* pulsation remain perceptible even though it becomes ever quieter and finally vanishes completely. The audible pulsation thus becomes a silent pulse—

the rhythmic foundation of everything we hear. The impact and the meaning of the rhythmic creations of the various bells and the *dondo*(talking-drum) are the result of the relationship with this perceptible but no longer audible pulsation.

Gankogui

Drum languages differ in their exactitude from one culture to another. The Brazilian samba uses a more or less free vocal imitation of various rhythm instruments. The correspondence between the drum and the vocal sounds is, however, clearly recognizable. The muffled and open blows used for different pitches and accents is audible in the vocal melody. In Example 17, you 17 will hear the improvised drum language of the samba—*a samba vocalizado*. These few examples of drum languages are a small part of the rich diversity existing in various cultures. They make clear the close relationship of drumming and rhythmic expression through speech.

In order to *speak through the drum,* sound patterns which correspond to words are played on the drum. This kind of drumming has developed primarily in cultures where a "tonal language" is spoken. In such a language, the meaning of a word is not only dependent on long and short, but also on the melodic ending of the words. For people who speak such a language, it is only natural that melodic drum rhythms would engender verbal associations. This has been systematically transposed onto the *talking drum.* A drum- 18 mer can thus play words that everyone understands. In Example 18, you can hear the drum language of the Ashanti people, played on a *dondo* by Ghanaian master drummer Aja Addy.

To *speak for a drum,* entails directing a mantra toward a specific drum. A drum can thus be charged with energy. This form of rhythmic language exists in all places where music plays an important part in healing ceremonies. The drums for which a mantra is recited serve ritual purposes. They are made from the wood of selected trees according to precisely prescribed rituals. In the act of making the drum, a profound relationship develops between the drummer and his instrument which later enables him to talk to his drum. Ritual drummers of many cultures have told me that a "being" dwells in such a drum, and I have seen ceremonies discontinued because the drum wouldn't "speak" on that particular day. No matter how one may conceive of such a "being," I have experienced how easily the playing of such drums put me into a trance. In that state of expanded perception, the mantra addressed to the drum quickly takes effect. I did not record an example of this drum language because the process described here is an experience of the moment. The examples presented in this chapter show that the ability to improvise rhythms with the voice is a fundamental precondition for truly inspired drumming. They also show us that the voice, as well as the drum, can help us reclaim the forgotten power of rhythm.

7

CREATING WITH THE ELEMENTS OF RHYTHM

I n every rhythm, we find elementary building blocks which, through their endless possibilities of combination, allow us to structure or form rhythm creatively. The most important elements and rhythmic building blocks have already been encountered: *pulsation, cycle, subdividing pulsation* as well as the five basic *off-beats*. When they become integrated as bodily feelings, you are ready to create rhythmic figures.

Creating a Rhythmic Figure

You have already experienced rhythmic structuring in previous chapters with *cycles* and *off-beats* which shape a pulsation in an elementary way. When we form rhythmic elements into complex figures we leave the archetypal realm of rhythm and enter the world of individual creation. Every culture has its characteristic rhythms which are either traditional (i.e. the result of musical interaction over time) or a more recent creation of a particular individual. These rhythms are not necessarily exclusive to a given culture—we find many identical and similar rhythms throughout the world.

A rhythmic figure has a set pattern or structure and a specific character which establishes its individuality. Rhythmic figures can be created in many ways. For example, if we clap a sequence of *off-beats,* always omitting the same one, we produce a simple rhythmic figure:

Clap	•	•	•	○	•	○	•	○	•	•	•	○	•	○	•	○
Voice	TA	KI	TA	KI	TA	KI	TA	KI	TA	KI	TA	KI	TA	KI	TA	KI
Step	<u>TA</u>		<u>KE</u>		<u>TI</u>		<u>NA</u>		<u>TA</u>		<u>KE</u>		<u>TI</u>		<u>NA</u>	

An explanation of the notation system used in this chapter can be found in Chapter 2, in the section "The Interaction of Clapping and Voice." The footstep outline used earlier, now appears as a dash (—). The syllables above the dash indicate the step. The vocal rhythm functions as a link between the claps and steps

Another form of rhythmic figure can be created by clapping on the first beat of every unit of a *nine beat* cycle.

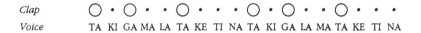

Clap

Voice TA KI GA MA LA TA KE TI NA TA KI GA LA MA TA KE TI NA

We enjoy an abundance of rhythmic figures because the possibilities for combining rhythmic elements are limitless. Each figure contains the archetypal movements of the rhythmic elements from which it is formed. When you clap the following figure with the TA KI step, feel how the movements of *beat, off-beat* and *double-time off-beat* are combined.

Clap

Voice TA KE TI NA TA KE TI NA TA KE TI NA TA KE TI NA

Step   TA   KI   TA   KI

Just as the off-beat is opposite the beat, so will every rhythmic figure have an opposite in its *complementary figure*. This complementary figure is composed of all the pulses which are left free in the original figure. We can think of it as the "shadow" of the original figure. Comprehension of a rhythmic figure is complete when we know its shadow. In the following exercise, try to experience the shadow after you have learned the basic figure.

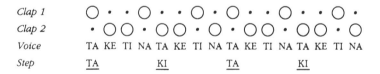

Clap 1

Clap 2

Voice TA KE TI NA TA KE TI NA TA KE TI NA TA KE TI NA

Step   TA   KI   TA   KI

Clap the two figures alternately to acquaint yourself with the difference in character. If you succeed in clapping one of the figures while speaking the other (with any syllables you choose), you will experience the two rhythms as a unity.

The Guideline

Certain rhythmic figures are played unvaryingly as a "fixed" figure which orients the musician and the listener, and also serves as a reference point for improvisation. These figures and their persistent repetition manifest a structural essence which guides the musician through the thicket of surrounding rhythms. Therefore they are called "guidelines" and they represent the essence of an individual rhythm.

Guidelines are usually played on instruments which have a clear and penetrating sound in order to "draw" rhythmic lines that cut through the sound of a whole ensemble. In Africa and Latin America, these are mainly bells and wooden sticks while in Asia guidelines are often played on gongs and small cymbals. Clapping, however, is the primal form of guideline and is found in every culture.

The most important guideline in Afro-Cuban music is produced by a simple expansion of the basic figure #3 (see Creating a Rhythmic Figure), using the elements of *beat, off-beat,* and *double-time off-beat.* The result is a four-beat cycle which you can experience by using the TA KE TI NA step.

```
Clap     O  ·  ·  O  ·  ·  O  ·  ·  ·  O  ·  O  ·  ·  ·
Voice    TA KE TI NA TA KE TI NA TA KE TI NA TA KE TI NA
Step     TA       KE       TI       NA
```

This guideline is known as *clave*—the key. It opens the door to a rhythmic understanding of the *rumba, salsa* and other forms of Afro-Cuban music. This guideline has two interchangeable parts. If the clave starts as you clapped it in the preceding example, then it is a 3/2 clave. Here is the reverse form, called a 2/3 clave:

```
Accented beats      1     2        1     2     3
Clap        ·  ·  O  ·  O  ·  ·  ·  O  ·  ·  O  ·  ·  O  ·
Voice       TA KE TI NA TA KE TI NA TA KE TI NA TA KE TI NA
Step        TA       KE       TI       NA
Basic pulse 1        2        3        4
```

The designation 3/2 or 2/3 indicates how many claps or strokes (when actually playing the claves) occur in each half of the four-beat cycle. In Latin America, Africa and Asia, we often find this method of counting only beats *actually played*, whereas in European music *all* of the ongoing basic beats are counted. By applying both concepts, we broaden our spectrum of musical comprehension.

The nature of the clave changes when one of its structural elements is altered. The third clap will generate more tension if we shift it from *off-beat* to *double-time off-beat*. This figure is called a *rumba clave* because it represents the rhythmic feeling in various forms of rumba. Try to clap this rumba clave with the TA KE TI NA step.

Clap	◯ · · ◯ · · · ◯ · · ◯ · ◯ · · ·
Voice	TA KE TI NA TA KE TI NA TA KE TI NA TA KE TI NA
Step	<u>TA</u> <u>KE</u> <u>TI</u> <u>NA</u>

This clave also exists in a 2/3 or reverse form. Frankie Malabie, one of the great Afro-Cuban percussionists, once said to me: "There is really only *one* clave. But some pieces of music begin with the *three* section and others with the *two* section."

The clave is more than a rhythmic figure—it is primarily a particular way of *feeling* rhythm. A musician playing Afro-Cuban music feels the clave even when it is not actually sounding. In recorded Example 19, you hear the clave figure played by a group at the Santiago de Cuba carnaval. The two percussion sticks used to play the clave figure are known as *claves*.

19

Claves

The unvarying rhythm of a guideline makes it a "pole of tranquility" amid the rhythmic process. The unchanging nature of a rhythmic figure over a long period can, however, easily lead to monotony and rigidity. A number of possibilities have therefore been developed for varying guidelines without changing their character and function. The following sections present some of these possibilities.

Embellishing a Guideline by Subdivision

In some Afro-Cuban rhythms, a second rhythmic figure with twice as many pulses as the clave is used. This rhythm, known as *cascara*, complements the character of the clave and is played with two sticks on the sides of a conga drum or a slit-drum known as *kata*. When *cascara* and *clave* are heard together a complex rhythm is created. It is interesting to listen for the points where the two rhythmic figures touch each other. Try to speak the *cascara* figure over the TA KE TI NA step. I've often heard the two syllables DAK and DU used in Cuba and Puerto Rico for vocal presentation of the *cascara*.

Voice	DAK • DU DAK • DAK • DU DAK • DAK • DA DAK • DU
Step	<u>TA</u> <u>KE</u> <u>TI</u> <u>NA</u>

Now try, on the same step, to clap the *rumba* clave while speaking the *cascara*. This will enable you to feel the interaction of the two guidelines.

Clap	◯ • • ◯ • • • ◯ • • ◯ • ◯ • • •
Voice	DAK • DU DAK • DAK • DU DAK • DAK • DA DAK • DU
Step	<u>TA</u> <u>KE</u> <u>TI</u> <u>NA</u>

Combined Guidelines

We can also vary a guideline without changing it by combining several parts. For example, several bells can be played together to form one guideline. Then, if a player omits a cycle while the others continue playing without any change, the impression is that the guideline varies. One of the musicians may also vary his part for a short time, but the constancy of the other parts will keep the guideline clear and recognizable. In Example 20, you

20

hear two double-bells, called *gonges* or *agogos*, playing a guideline together. I made this recording of an *afoxe* (pronounced afóshay) group playing an *ijexa* rhythm during the 1980 carnaval at Salvador/Bahia. Groups such as "Filhos de Gandhi" and "Ile Aye" comprise several hundred dancers and musicians performing *afoxes* and *maraçatus* which are the most important forms of Afro-Brazilian music during carnaval. In these groups, a guideline can involve up to twenty different elements which, although continually varied by the number and type of figures played, nonetheless retain their original feeling and shape.

The following exercise allows you to experience both parts of the *agogo* guideline:

> Begin slowly with the TA KE TI NA step and when you feel you have found your own tempo, sub-divide all the intervals in the basic step by vocalizing TA KE TI NA. Now on the foundation established by voice and step, start to clap as follows:

Clap	○ · ○ · ○ · ○ · ○○ · ○ · ○○ ·
Voice	TA KE TI NA TA KE TI NA TA KE TI NA TA KE TI NA
Step	<u>TA</u> <u>KE</u> <u>TI</u> <u>NA</u>

This is one fundamental pattern of the *ijexa* guideline. You can make its "melody" audible by gradually letting the vocal TA KE TI NA become ever quieter while continuing to step and clap. Now clap the guideline and vocalize the syllables TIN, TI, GO and RO as shown here.

Clap	○ · ○ · ○ · ○ · ○○ · ○ · ○○ ·
Voice	TIN TIN GO GO TI TIN GO GO RO
Step	<u>TA</u> <u>KE</u> <u>TI</u> <u>NA</u>

Using the same step, you can now try the second part of the guideline. The sub-dividing pulsation is also TA KE TI NA. If you find it easier, return to speaking TA KE TI NA before clapping.

Clap	· · ○○○ · ○○ · ○ · ○ · ○○ ·
Voice	TI TI TIN GO GO TIN GO GO RO
Step	<u>TA</u> <u>KE</u> <u>TI</u> <u>NA</u>

This is the rhythm of guideline #1, divided into *high* and *low* sounds.

Bell 1

This is the rhythm of guideline #2 divided into *high* and *low* sounds.

Bell 2

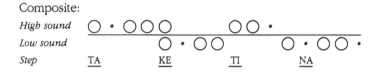

This is how bells 1 and 2 sound when played together.

Composite:

High sound				
Low sound				
Step	TA	KE	TI	NA

Guideline Embellishment Using Added Variations

Another possibility for freeing the rigid form of a guideline is to orna-ment it with ongoing variations played on one or two other instruments. The guideline itself remains unchanged, but the overall sound now exhibits a greater variety of color. Example 21 is from a recording I made during a shamanic ceremony in Korea, which was conducted by Kim Sok Chul and his group. The guideline itself is played on a the *tsching,* which often func-tions in this manner. The ornamentation is played on the *guengari* and the bass membrane of the *tschanggo* drum. The *tsching* and *guengari* are also used in Korean classical music as sound instruments and are called *sokum* (little iron) and *taekum* (big iron). In the music of the shamans, however, they have become guideline instruments. The guideline played on the *tsching* is a simple figure derived from a three-beat cycle.

21

Guengari

Tsching	◊	•	◆	◊	◆	•	◊	•	◆	◊	◆	•
Steps	GA		MA		LA		GA		MA		LA	

One Guideline Set Into Different Cycles

A very effective way of altering the rhythmic quality of a guideline without changing it, is to play this same rhythmic figure on foundations of different cycles. This is possible whenever a guideline contains a number of pulses which can be divided into different but equal groups. Twelve, for example, can be divided as follows:

Divided into 2 equal parts: 6 + 6 = 12
Divided into 3 equal parts: 4 + 4 + 4 = 12
Divided into 4 equal parts: 3 + 3 + 3 + 3 = 12
Divided into 6 equal parts: 2 + 2 + 2 + 2 + 2 + 2 = 12

As the number of possible divisions increases, we gain more forms of the same guideline. As an example, let's use one of the most important guidelines in African music. You can try it by first speaking the syllables TIN and GO.

Voice   TIN • GO • GO GO • GO • GO • GO

Notice that this figure repeats after twelve pulses. When would you step while clapping this guideline? In the simplest case, you could step on *every* pulse which would then be a twelve-beat cycle. However, this is only possible at a very slow tempo, and therefore not used, although theoretically possible. Since we must use fewer steps as the guideline tempo is increased, you can, in the following example, see the relationship of the step to voice (or clap) as you step at the division of two, three, four or six.

Clap	○	•	○	•	○○	•	○	•	○	•	○
Voice	TIN	•	GO	•	GOGO	•	GO	•	GO	•	GO
1. Step	TA	•	•	•	•	•	KI	•	•	•	•
2. Step	GA	•	•	•	MA	•	•	•	LA	•	•
3. Step	TA	•	•	KE	•	•	TI	•	•	NA	•
4. Step	GA	•	MA	•	LA	•	GA	•	MA	•	LA

Each time the step changes, a new foundation is produced, which changes not only the way we hear the guideline, but also the rhythmic feeling in the body. In Example 22, you will first hear the undivided guideline played on an African bell with the first beat played on a lower pitched bell. Then the *moktak* enters and divides the cycle into two equal parts, then three, four and six parts. Following that are eight and nine beat cycles which are created by sub-dividing the twelve beats. This produces very complex rhythms which exhibit an exciting tension. The following exercise enables you to experience these changes.

22

Begin the TA KE TI NA step at a tempo that allows you to easily speak the three syllables GA MA LA between each step. When the movement of the step enables you to feel the four-beat cycle, gradually begin to speak the GA MA LA sequence making sure that the three syllables equally divide the interval between each step. When your step and voice flow together smoothly, you can make the guideline audible by clapping as follows:

Clap	○	•	○	•	○○	•	○	•	○	•	○
Voice	GA MA LA		GA MA LA		GA MA LA		GA MA LA				
Step	TA		KE		TI		NA				

You have now experienced the guideline as a four-beat cycle. You can feel the rhythmic structure of the guideline even more clearly by gradually silencing the vocal GA MA LA and replace it with the two syllables TIN and GO as previously used.

Clap	○ · ○ · ○○ · ○ · ○ · ○
Voice	TIN GO GO GO GO GO GO
Step	<u>TA</u> <u>KE</u> <u>TI</u> <u>NA</u>

Now, let your steps get smaller and smaller and gradually come to a stop but continue the guideline with your clapping and voice. When you feel ready, change the spoken syllables to TA KI.

Clap	○ · ○ · ○○ · ○ · ○ · ○
Voice	<u>TA</u> KI TA <u>KI</u> TA KI <u>TA</u> KI TA <u>KI</u> TA KI

Allow yourself time to sense how the clapping and voice interact and when you feel secure begin to step on every TA. Now you feel the guideline on the new foundation. You will feel the power of the entire six-beat cycle by walking in place using the GA MA LA step.

Clap	○ · ○ · ○○ · ○ · ○ · ○
Voice	TA KI TA KI TA KI TA KI TA KI TA KI
Step	<u>GA</u> <u>MA</u> <u>LA</u> <u>GA</u> <u>MA</u> <u>LA</u>

22   In the second part of Example 22, you hear this guideline at a faster tempo played on an African *dondo* and on Korean *sambuks*. Even though the guideline is not always played, its structure can be clearly perceived. This guideline is an important component of African music and is the backbone of many rhythms, especially those used in rituals. Africans brought this rhythm to Brazil, where it became an important energy in the *candomble* ceremony and to Cuba where it is used in the *santeria* rituals. Music plays a central role in both candomble and santeria which are effective rituals for the healing of mental and physical suffering. We also find this guideline in many forms of jazz where it has broadened the awareness of drummers and percussionists and given a vital impetus to existing rhythmic concepts. When I discovered a slight variation of the same guideline in Korea, a series of relationships was completed for me. Here I found, uninfluenced by other cultures, the same twelve-beat structure that I had encountered in the ritual music of Africa, Brazil and Cuba. In Korea, it is the most important rhythm of the shamans who use it as a guideline for the rhythm known as *salpuri* which can be translated as "purification." This guideline is primarily used where psychological impact is the central consideration. This impact is generated by the rhythmic power of the twelve-beat cycle, which, as we have seen, can be divided into many different parts. In rituals using this guideline, the participants are affected both physically and psychologically by the nuances of the various cycles.

Each new division of the cycle may be likened to an additional overtone in the harmonic series, which we examined in Chapter 5. The guideline also takes on a new character every time a new division occurs. The twelve-beat cycle divided into three equal parts has a wholly different quality than a division of four equal parts. This holds true for an unstructured cycle as well as a figure of twelve-beats.

The structure is only one aspect of a rhythmic figure however. The other involves the endless possibilities of drum sounds which we can use to play a rhythmic figure. To vary a rhythmic figure we can either change its rhythmic form or leave the form unchanged and vary the figure using different drum sound "melodies." The endless sonic possibilities offered by the drum and other percussion instruments present an unlimited palette of variations.

8

SONIC AND CREATIVE POSSIBILITIES OF PERCUSSION

The tonal character of a percussion instrument is shaped by its method of construction, materials used, and the way it is played. The particular sound-spectrum of each instrument will determine how it affects us. The boom of a bass drum affects a different level of our consciousness and our body than the high tones of a rattle. The sonic possibilities of each instrument dictate its rhythmic function. For instance, the variations a *guengari* player uses to embellish the *tsching* guideline would sound confusing and out of place on a slit-drum. The *guengari*, in turn, has a sound not suited for clean delineation of a rhythmic figure. A simple, unvaried guideline sounds crude on this instrument.

The Power of Percussive Sound

To watch a child play with a rattle, marvelling with mouth open and in direct contact with the sound, is to witness the powerful effect sound has on our consciousness. Certain musical instruments have the ability to uncover layers of awareness long forgotten and bring us into a deeper contact with the self.

In his investigations, Tomatis has discovered that high frequencies, such as the sound of a rattle, supply the cerebral cortex with the electric charge necessary to stimulate certain levels of consciousness. When I hear a rattle play a regular rhythm for an extended period of time, it has a clarifying and vitalizing effect on me. This sound resonates in the upper parts of my body and head.

Caxixi

Deep sounds, on the other hand, such as the resonance of a bass drum, act primarily on our organs of balance and generate an impulse toward movement. While playing in a Brazilian samba group, I experienced the sound of the *surdos* as an actual rhythmic movement in my body and as I danced and played I felt myself being carried by their sound. My involvement with a variety of instruments has taught me that we can listen with the whole body. I have also discovered that certain sounds always speak to the same part of my body.

Some Possibilities for Drum Creativity

The multitude of drums opens up an abundance of sonic possibilities. On the one hand, we can use them to create audible pulsations, cycles, and sub-dividing beats, while on the other, we can employ drums to freely create on the rhythmic foundation of a silent pulse and a weight pattern. The endless number of rhythms results from the unlimited creative possibilities of the great variety of percussion combinations. We can shape rhythm by linking rhythmic structure with a specific drum "melody." There are essentially five possibilities, ranging from free to restricted:

1. The least structured form is a *recitative speaking* using drum sounds. It is limited only by the coherence and tension produced by the phrases. Recitative drumming can engender an exciting dialogue between musicians.

2. *Improvisation* is the form of creation that offers the greatest freedom whenever one plays on the foundation of a regular pulsation. A drummer may combine all existing elements in his creation, or even abandon the pulsation and other rhythmic foundations as long as he continues to hear the underlying pulse and weight pattern in order to return to the established structure. By abandoning the supportive relationship of the silent pulse, tension-generating lines are created. Improvisation usually occurs as a solo whether the musician is actually playing alone or as a soloist in an ensemble.

3. *Variation* is a form which requires the musician to vary the *"theme" supplied by a rhythmic figure*. No matter how this is accomplished, the original form of the rhythmic figure should always remain apparent. This form also requires the musician to adhere to the foundation of pulsation and cycle. After a concert together in Rio de Janeiro, I asked my Brazilian friend Djalma Correa how he managed to vary difficult rhythmic figures with such ease, and he replied: "I play the basic form of a rhythmic figure until it varies itself."

4. The *persistent "drum melody" (ostinato)* is a form of lesser creative freedom. If we reduce it to its most basic level we find we have essentially four sounds that can be created on the skin of a drum: muffled and open sounding, high and low. An open tone however can vary from a resonant sound full of overtones to a short, dry sound. On a skin, the "high" sound is produced by hitting the drum so that more overtones are produced. A slap on a conga, for example, has a considerably higher tone than an open sound. Of course, the way a drum is built determines its sonic possibilities: a tabla enables the player to bring out more variations than a more primitive "native" drum. A drum that is played with the hands usually allows much more subtle sound variations than a stick drum. All the sounds we've experienced in percussive languages are available for the creation of drum figures and

"melodies." If we play the same rhythmic figure with two different sequences of sounds, its impact will change. The sequence of drum sounds used in playing a rhythmic figure is a structuring component. Every rhythm has a combination of drum sounds which make audible its basic structure. This combination corresponds to the guideline and creates an unvarying element which serves as both a pole of tranquility and a source of orientation. However, this basic "melody" also serves as an effective way of remembering a rhythm. More about this is presented in the following section, "Basic Forms of a Drum Melody."

5. The generation of a simple rhythmic foundation offers the least creative freedom. An alternation of a muffled and open sound on the *surdo* will produce a two-beat cycle. This simple melodic form cannot be considered a rhythmic figure. If we call the muffled sound TAK and the resonant, open sound DUM, then the "melody" is:

Voice	TAK	•	•	•	DUM	•	•	•	TAK	•	•	•	DUM	•	•	•
Inner Voice	TA	KE	TI	NA	TA	KE	TI	NA	TA	KE	TI	NA	TA	KE	TI	NA
Step	TA				KI				TA				KI			

A simple extension makes this cyclical structure into an elementary rhythmic figure:

Voice	TAK	•	•	GU	DUM	•	•	GA	TAK	•	•	GU	DUM	•	•	GA
Inner Voice	TA	KE	TI	NA	TA	KE	TI	NA	TA	KE	TI	NA	TA	KE	TI	NA
Step	TA				KI				TA				KI			

Filling the free pulses with other sounds, you produce a basic *samba* figure:

Voice	TA	G	TSCH	GU	DU	M	TSCH	GA	TA	G	TSCH	GU	DU	M	TSCH	GA
Inner Voice	TA	KE	TI	NA	TA	KE	TI	NA	TA	KE	TI	NA	TA	KE	TI	NA
Step	TA				KI				TA				KI			

Of course, there are also combinations of these five basic forms of rhythmic creativity.

Basic Forms of a Drum Melody

In all cultures, we find that the most basic form of any drum rhythm is associated with a certain drum "melody," (sequence of drum sounds) which helps us recognize a specific rhythm. In Indian music, the basic form of the drum "melody" is called *theka*. You are already acquainted with the *chautal theka*—a combination of *bolas* which characterize this rhythm. When a *tabla* player accompanies another musician, he plays virtually nothing but a slightly varied form of *theka*. Only during his solo does he improvise. By hearing the *theka* sequence of syllables within himself he can improvise effortlessly over long cycles.

When I studied in Korea, I found it very confusing that a particular rhythm was sometimes called *tongtongi* and sometimes *tscha tschin kutkori* or *tscha tschin mori* and that none of the musicians, who were such masterly exponents of these rhythms, could explain their structure to me. One day, a musician friend, who had long lived with shamans, told me that neither the name, nor the structure of a rhythm, was important in the shamanic tradition. The rhythms were passed on from father to son through a drum language. Actual experience in the ceremonies gave an apprentice the opportunity to hear the rhythms and their variations. A rhythm's underlying "melody" is known in Korea as *tschom su*. Knowing the *tschom su* enables the musician to recognize a rhythm immediately; therefore, it doesn't matter if the same rhythm has three different names.

In Latin America, we also find an underlying form of drum "melody." In Brazil it is simply known as the *base do ritmo* and in Cuba and Puerto Rico as *tumbao*. You can experience a simple *tumbao* in the following exercise.

Begin the exercise with the TA KE TI NA step. When you sense the pulsation and cycle of your steps, speak a TA KE TI NA with your *inner voice* for *each* step. While you hear this inner TA KE TI NA, try to speak the following rhythmic figure aloud:

Voice	•	•	BAK	•	•	•	GU	GU	•	•	BAK	•	•	•	GU	GU
Inner Voice	TA	KE	TI	NA	TA	KE	TI	NA	TA	KE	TI	NA	TA	KE	TI	NA
Step	<u>TA</u>				<u>KE</u>				<u>TI</u>				<u>NA</u>			

When you feel secure clap the *clave* figure. Now you can feel how the *clave* and *tumbao* interact:

Clap	O	•	•	O	•	•	O	•	•	•	O	•	O	•	•	•
Voice	•	•	BAK	•	•	•	GU	GU	•	•	BAK	•	•	•	GU	GU
Inner Voice	TA	KE	TI	NA	TA	KE	TI	NA	TA	KE	TI	NA	TA	KE	TI	NA
Step	<u>TA</u>				<u>KE</u>				<u>TI</u>				<u>NA</u>			

Drum Melodies in an Ensemble

Since drum "melodies" combine when several drums and other percussion instruments are played in ensemble, the tuning of the drums is very important. The "melodies," like the rhythmic structures, have to work together. Certain rhythmic figures support and strengthen when sounding together, while others may interfere with one another. This principle also applies to the way drum melodies sound together. Every culture has contributed to the rich tradition of the percussion ensemble in its own unique way. Nevertheless, certain universal principles based on acoustical laws apply, regardless of cultural tastes and disposition. If an instrument's frequency range is spread across an ensemble, its rhythm becomes more transparent. But if the chief concern is the fusing of several figures, then the sound and frequency range of the drums needs to be similar. Guidelines must be played on penetrating instruments, but an accompanying figure would sound excessive on the same instruments. The drum itself determines how successfully it combines with other instruments. Some are better in small ensembles or in solo roles, while others only unfold their full power in a larger group.

23 In Example 23, I present a Cuban *comparsa*—an ensemble of about forty drummers who combine various rhythmic figures to form a single rhythm. I made this recording during the 1979 carnaval in Santiago de Cuba. You can hear alternating rhythmic figures, both varying and constant. Try to speak one of these figures. The *comparsa* consists primarily of *congas, bombos* (large bass drums), and bells. You will also hear a wind instrument similar to one used in the Korean shaman ceremony. This Asian instrument is known in Korea as a *hojak*, in India as *shenai*, and in Cuba as *trompeta de china*.

Cuban comparsa (carnaval Santiago de Cuba)

Drums I Play: Their Symbolic Character—
Their Energy Fields

For me, the drum is a being of rhythmic power whose nature is revealed to me as I play it. Each drum speaks to a different part of me. Some drums —such as the *tschanggo*, the *pakhavaj* and the *tabla*—affect my left-right consciousness. Others, such as the Korean *buk* or the Japanese *taiko*, immediately bring me to the center of my body and the power that lies there. The *conga* and *atabaque* have helped me discover a well-grounded power within myself, and when I play the *surdo* I am able to feel myself being carried by the rhythm.

The drum returns my energy by transforming it into audible rhythm and thus completes a circuit of an energy field which allows me to connect with my own power. In what follows, I would like to tell you about the kind of directional energy I have experienced with various drums, and the physical and spiritual connections they brought about. I will confine myself to the drums with which I have had extensive experience. The feeling of being rhythmically carried is a central theme in the playing of a drum. All drums confront the player with the independence of left and right and require us to access the power in the center of our body. Nevertheless, each drum has its own primary theme and therefore, its own special fascination.

Buk and Taiko—Centering and a Counterpart

Buk and Taiko: Leonard Eto (Kodo) and Reinhard Flatischler

Both the Korean *buk* and the Japanese *taiko* are barrel-drums. A skin is stretched on both ends of a cylindrical or bulging wooden body. This drum came from China and was brought to Korean zen monasteries and thence to Japan where the *taiko* was developed. The *buk* and *taiko* have helped me find my physical center and unite it with the power that dwells there. This has enabled me to deploy the heavy beaters with an ease that allows the entire drum to vibrate. When I play the *buk*, I experience it as an alter ego—more so than any other drum. One stands to play the *buk*, which is at eye level and this position involves the whole body in a kind of drumming dance.

On the small island of Sado off the west coast of Honshu, there lives a group of *taiko* drummers who are the most recent heirs of a thousand year-old tradition. They have become famous across the world as the *Kodo* group. These musicians link the heart-beat of ancient Japanese drum tradition with their own creative arrangements in an uncompromising affirmation of the power of drumming. The characteristic sound of the barrel-drum is a robust bass reverberation which can be clearly felt in the chest and stomach. Listening to a large *buk*, we feel the sound fill the entire body.

Conga and Atabaque—Earth-Directed Power

Atabaque (Salvador Bahia)

The *conga* and *atabaque* are drums whose energy flows vertically toward the earth. The drummer's hand contacts the skin and thus creates a direct and immediate energy path. The slightest change in hand position brings about a new sound. The *conga*, as I experience it, is more a part of my body than a counterpart, as is the *buk*. As I learned this drum, I saw that the space between the hand and the earth is the *conga's* energy field. The *buk* generates forward movement whereas the *conga's* energy-flow goes directly toward the earth.

In Africa and Latin America, there are innumerable forms of this drum which all have the downward flow of energy. Each has its own tonal character depending on whether the body is made out of a single piece of wood or several elements, whether it is open or closed at the bottom and whether it is slender or bulbous in shape. This type of drum is phallic in appearance and playing it activates my male energy more than any other.

Tschanggo, Pakhavaj, and Batá–
Consciousness of the Interaction of Left and Right

Before I present the *tschanggo, pakhavaj,* and *batá,* I'd like to introduce the Asian prototype of a drum which unites two polarities. It is called the *damaru,* and I first encountered it at the Dalai Lama's monastery at Dharmsala. The *damaru* consists of the tops of two human skulls—one female, one male. These skull-tops are joined together at the vertex and covered with human skin. Two cords, with small bones attached to the ends, are fixed where the skulls meet. TAK TAK TAK TAK....a unique penetrating sound emerges whenever the drum is rotated back and forth, a sound that reaches deep within us. With each TAK, male and the female are united as both bones strike the two sides simultaneously. This symbolism is also to be found in similar form in the Korean *tschanggo* (see photo on page 112). The two "shells" of the wooden body correspond to the two skulls. The main body is, however, made from a single hollow piece of wood with both ends open so that when one membrane is struck the other also resonates. The left-hand skin of the *tschanggo* is called *kungpjön,* which means "Gateway to the Hereafter" and the right hand skin *tschepjön,* "Gateway to This World." The sound resulting from beating either membrane unites both ends. *Kungpjön* and *tschepjön* correspond to the two halves of the body. The left arm movement is linked with the right half of the brain and with this the *tschanggo* player beats at the "gateway to the world of the holistic and intuitive." The right side of the body is connected with the analyzing, rational left half of the brain and with this the musician knocks at the "gateway to the world of structured waking consciousness." When I play the *tschanggo* an awareness of the interconnected movements between the two halves of my body and brain is stimulated. The energy flow in the *tschanggo* is horizontal as it moves from one skin to the other. The *tschanggo,* more than any other drum, speaks to my feminine side.

Two Indian drums, the *pakhavaj* and the *mridangam,* also have this type of energy flow. They are played with both hands and here too when one membrane is struck the other vibrates. The sound of the two skins unites in the drum's wooden body, which then becomes highly resonant. *Pakhavaj* means "the sound of bird's wings" and is evocative of the feeling created when the drummer playing the *pakhavaj* takes "flight." Beating the drum at both ends allows a feeling of great freedom to develop in the arms. The origins of the *pakhavaj* are symbolically described in the following legend:

Pakhavaj
(Pandit Arjun Shejwal)

Upon conquering a demon, Shiva was overjoyed and began to dance so vigorously that the earth shook. People feared that the end of the world had come. But when Ganesha saw Shiva dancing he formed a drum body from the bloody earth around the demon. From the demon's skin, he made the membrane and from his innards the drum binding. He thus created the first *pakhavaj.* When Ganesha had completed this instrument he began to accompany Shiva's dance. His playing gradually became slower and in this way he was able to calm Shiva down with the *pakhavaj.* Peace and tranquility were restored to humankind.

Tabla—A Combination of Two Principles

Today, the *tabla* is the most important drum in North Indian music. This pair of drums combines two principles. It's as if a *pakhavaj* were split in half with the left end then becoming the *bayan* and the right, the higher sounding *dayan.* The left-right configuration is preserved, but the direction of playing is now (as with the *conga*) toward the earth—and this gives the *tabla* a wholly different quality than the *pakhavaj.* This difference allows the *tabla*-player to change the membrane tension on the bass drum by using the palm of his hand and in this way play the *bayan* melodically.

Drum Ensembles

The *pakhavaj* is a solo drum, while the *batá* is always played in ensemble. Certain drums, such as the *surdo, batá, atabaque* and *conga* only unfold their full power in ensemble. Others, such as the *tabla* or *pakhavaj,* have a greater impact when played solo. Of course, there are also mixed forms, allowing for both solo and ensemble playing. The most common drum ensemble is a trio.

The *batá* has three forms: the *iyá, itótele* and *okónkolo.* The *iyá* or "mother drum" gives the "calls" for rhythmic changes. The *iyá* thus initiates the rhythm and plays variations mostly on the deeper membrane.

When I began my study of Latin American music, it was unclear to me why the highest drum in a *rumba* ensemble took the solos while the *batás* and Brazilian *atabaques* gave that role to the deepest drum. As I gained experience with these drums, I learned that variations played on the deeper drums affect deeper levels of my consciousness, whereas solos on high-pitched drums create a completely different atmosphere—one of extroversion and the desire for movement. The *iyá* is the lead instrument in the bata ensemble. It has the greatest freedom for imporvisation and gives all the important "calls." The *itótele* player answers these calls and makes occasional improvisations. With his ongoing rhythm, he interlocks perfectly with the *okónkolo,* the smallest drum in the ensemble. Its role is to mark the subdividing pulsation with an unvaried rhythmic figure. The rhythms of the three drums are so intertwined that all membranes together produce a full-fledged "melody" that completely unifies the *iyá, itótele,* and *okónkolo.*

Three different drums of the same family playing together are common in many kinds of music. The *rumba,* for example, has three musicians playing on different size *congas* the *quinto* (high), *conga* (middle) and *tumbadora* (low). The Brazilian *atabaque* also exists in three sizes: *rum, rumpi,* and *le* (pronounced hum, humpi and le). *Le* is the smallest, *rum* the largest. Size, however, accounts for only one aspect. In a group of three drums, there is also the distribution of various rhythmic functions. In solo playing, complexity develops mainly through the creation of extensive phrases and the combination of many sonic possibilities. But in an ensemble of similar drums, various figures merge into a single rhythm. One drummer can play a solo while the others maintain regular patterns.

There are also three different *surdo* functions in a *samba* ensemble. The *chamado* calls, which means that it presents the higher-sounding beat and the *reposta* answers with a low boom. These two mark the *samba's* pulsation and two-beat cycle and are therefore also called *surdo marcacão*. The *centrador* connects those two with a variety of rhythmic figures. It is, so to speak, the solo drum in the *surdo* ensemble. In a *bateria* (a large *samba* ensemble) all three *surdo* functions are carried out by a number of players. Up to sixty *surdos* play together in the big *samba* schools.

Each culture produces its own unique drums and rhythms. When I began my journey into rhythm, I endeavored to play as "authentically" as possible. At that time, I viewed authenticity as playing an accurate imitation of the rhythms I had learned. However, as time passed it became clear to me that true authenticity comes from two sources. The first is a deep study of each drum's rhythms within its own tradition. The other source, however, is one's personal vision of rhythm which engenders the creation of new rhythmic compositions and one's personal approach to improvising, as well as the energy field that one creates while drumming. When I composed my first creative rhythms, I noticed how the different ways of playing various drums stimulated my ideas. It then became clear that the knowledge of world rhythms and authentic playing techniques I had acquired on all these drums would lead me toward a discovery of my own drumming style.

Bateria in "Carnaval Da Rua" 1980, Rio de Janeiro

9

CLOSING WORDS

The path to rhythm consciousness, to which I invited you at the beginning of this book, is without end. I thank you for allowing me to guide you through the various aspects, energies and appearances of rhythm. We have now reached a point where I must say goodbye and allow you to continue on your own. Your personal learning tempo will determine when the various rhythmic energies become part of your rhythmic body awareness. To me, this tempo is part of one's personality, and heeding it will enable you to experience whatever is valuable for you

You may want to memorize some of the exercises in this book that have been joyful and exciting and use them for your daily practice. Be encouraged to experiment with the interaction of step, clap, and voice in a variety of life situations. The exercises with your body will provide you with a solid foundation for continuing your development on percussion instruments and drums. Guideline instruments such as rattles, bells and claves are ideal instruments to integrate into the TA KE TI NA exercises.

At the end of your exercises, as you let your steps get smaller and smaller, listen inside yourself: if you sense the silent pulse continuing within, you may be ready to play a drum. Whether you learn to play ten drums or only one, you will enter a path without end, and discover that the journey itself is the essential experience. As your rhythmic body-awareness develops during this process, you will begin to see many possibilities for combining different kinds of drums.

The vast number of drum types in the world exceeds comprehension. It doesn't seem possible that one could know all the drums within a single culture, let alone be able to play them. I believe, however, that the important thing is not which drum you learn, but *how* you learn it and how it relates to your life. I also believe that the path of drumming requires a personal teacher who is capable of reaching your inner self with his or her knowledge. In this way, drumming will become an integrated part of your daily life, a source of power and a place for recreation.

24 The various drums I play still seem to me like pieces in a mosaic. Many sonic images have developed as I tried to assemble the pieces. Example 24 presents one of these.

The above image can be seen as a "rhythm mandala" and represents a form of notation as well. The petals symbolize the pulses, and it is easy to see that this is a joint cycle of six and nine beats. While you are looking at the mandala, listen to the rhythm and let image and sound combine in your perception.

With this final musical example, I encourage you to set out in search of your own creative rhythms. It could be that with your first rhythmic creation you will discover an unknown part of your musical self.

REINHARD FLATISCHLER

• Born 1950 in Vienna

• Piano diploma at the Music University Vienna

• Many years of drumstudies in Asia and Latin America

• Teaches at many universities and institutions around the world

• Member of Scientific Committee in the International Society for Music in Medicine

• Founder of the institute for rhythmeducation and rhythmresearch

• Leader of the project „Rhythm and Pain Therapy", conducted together with Dr. Schwefe, director of the German Society for Pain Therapy

• Rhythm coach for major companies

• Leader and composer of the MegaDrums group, that includes musician like Airto Moreira, Zakir Hussain, Glen Velez, Milton Cardona, Stephen Kent and Leonard Eto (Kodo)

"TaKeTiNa is an essential contribution for the evolution of music-pedagogics."
Prof. W. Hasitschka
[Rector of the Music University in Vienna]

"TaKeTiNa is powerful, playful, earthy, and yet transcendent - very inspiring!"
Deva Premal & Miten
[Spiritual singers and songwriters]

"TaKeTiNa is healing, especially for people, suffering from psychosomatic diseases."
Dr. med. G. Müller-Schwefe
[chairman of the German Society for Paintherapy]

"It is a honor to be part of Flatischlers musical work."
Airto Moreira
[Master Percussionist (Miles Davis, Chick Corea)]

RECORDED MUSICAL EXAMPLES

1.	Pulsation	Recorded in the Pulgug-Sa Zen monastery in Korea	2:46
2.	Munmyochereak	Recorded at the Confucian temple in Seoul, Korea	2:20
3.	March and Samba	Vençeremos, Samba de roda	1:56
4.	GA MA LA TA KI a five-beat cycle	R. Flatischler: tsching, tschanggo, moktak,tambourim, bell, vocal	3:05
5.	The Sub-Division of the Interval	R. Flatischler: surdo, foot rattle, berimbão, vocal	2:59
6.	The Five Basic Off-Beats	R. Flatischler: surdo, foot rattle, berimbão, moktak, vocal	4:53
7.	The Joint Cycle of 2 and 3	R. Flatischler: surdo, foot rattle, berimbão, moktak, vocal	2:17
8.	Additive & Divisive Cycles: Structuring a joint cycle of six and nine beats	R. Flatischler: rantang, bells, gongs	2:33
9.	Seven Pitch Intervals	R. Flatischler: monochord	3:48
10.	Overtone Singing	R. Flatischler: vocal, overtone tubes, sound bowls, waterphone	3:47
11.	The GA MA LA Step	R. Flatischler: surdo, foot rattle, tschanggo, berimbão, moktak, tambourim, vocal	3:04
12.	The TA KE TI NA Step	R. Flatischler: surdo, foot rattle, congas, berimbão, moktak, cuica,vocal	3:30
13.	Tala: Clapping the Rhythmic Foundation	Pandit Arjun Shejwal: pakhavaj	2:08

14.	Indian Drum Language	a) R. Flatischler: tabla, vocal b) Pandit Arjun Shejwal: pakhavaj, vocal	3:15
15.	Korean Drum Language	R. Flatischler: tschanggo, vocal	2:22
16.	African Percussive Language/The Silent Pulse	Aja Addy: dondo R. Flatischler: gankoguis, moktak, vocal	3:34
17.	Brazilian Percussion Language	Luciano Perrone: vocal	0:59
18.	African Drum Language Spoken Through a Drum	Aja Addy: dondo, vocal	1:52
19.	Clave Guideline	Recorded at the 1979 carnaval in Santiago de Cuba	2:24
20.	Ijexa Guideline	Recorded at the 1981 carnaval in Salvador/Bahia	2:07
21.	Tsching Guideline	Recorded at a Korean shamanic "Kut"ceremony (Dong Hean O-Gui Kut)	3:14
22.	Guideline Set Into Different Cycles	a) R. Flatischler: gankogui, moktak,surdo b) Aja Addy: dondo R. Flatischler: sambuk	7:37
23.	Rhythmic Figures of a Comparsa	Recorded at the 1979 carnaval in Santiago de Cuba	3:06
24.	Rhythm Mosaic 6:9	R. Flatischler: conga, batá, caxixi, bell, vocal	3:33

TaKeTiNa - 40 years of music, education, therapy and research

TaKeTiNa is a process for activating human and musical potential through rhythm. TaKeTiNa conveys rhythm in the manner that people naturally grasp and learn it: by direct physical experience of fundamental rhythmic movement. The capacity for this is inborn; all infants come into the world with the sensory and motor skills that become the rhythmic foundation of all music.

TaKeTiNa combines the rhythmic knowledge found in ancient cultures together with modern findings from the fields of music, rhythmic research, cybernetics, communication, neurological research and chaos theory. The result is a new form of human and musical learning. TaKeTiNa is just as appropriate for musical laypersons as for professional musicians.

Because the TaKeTiNa process is based on deep and multifaceted experience, it can only be led by trained TaKeTiNa teachers. You can, however, get to know the TaKeTiNa process using this book or the TaKeTiNa book "Rhythm for Evolution".

In daily life, TaKeTiNa can help you:

- relax more deeply
- stay focused for an exceptionally long time
- deal creatively and effectively with chaotic phases
- lessen your anxiety about mistakes and thus, help you make fewer mistakes
- perceive several things simultaneously

TaKeTiNa can be used by musicians to:

- stay in the groove
- develop profound rhythmic orientation
- develop improvisatory and compositional abilities
- expand competence on drums and percussion instruments

TaKeTiNa in the elementary musical field

TaKeTiNa enables beginners to comprehend and put basic rhythmic elements into practice using "learning by doing". Countless people have begun playing music as a result of Reinhard Flatischler's work, many of whom would otherwise never have taken up an instrument. Experiencing TaKeTiNa shows participants that rhythm is an elementary force of life that everyone can tap into.

Learning at many levels is the prerequisite for a profound understanding of fundamental rhythmic movements: offbeats, cycles and polyrhythmic structures are experienced and comprehended even without any understanding of musical notation.

TaKeTiNa in the professional musical field

With his new perspective on rhythm and the musical style that developed from it, Reinhard Flatischler has influenced generations of younger musicians. His MegaDrums project proved that even the world's best musicians are inspired by his new manner of composition and use it to express themselves in an outstanding manner. Many professional musicians have deepened their abilities and knowledge in Reinhard Flatischler's numerous drumming and percussion courses.

TaKeTiNa is an outstanding method for learning to improvise and compose; it opens up paths for creating one's own rhythms as well. It provides a versatile setting for musicians to further develop their abilities on their own instruments. This method involves the entire body as well as the voice. The results are remarkable, not only for jazz or classical musicians, but also for world musicians, because they greatly strengthen groove, flow, orientation and the capacity for individual expression. TaKeTiNa likewise provides comprehensive training for further developing left-right coordination and independence.

Therapeutical and social work-based uses of TaKeTiNa

Since TaKeTiNa activates deep inner processes, it can be used to enhance therapeutic work in client settings. TaKeTiNa is currently used with great success in pain management, psychotherapy, psychosomatic rehabilitation and with drug addicts.

TaKeTiNa rhythm research

For over two decades, Reinhard Flatischler has been involved in rhythm research in connection with a number of universities and research institutes. He began his cooperation with Dr. Koepchen in the Society for Music in Medicine, following this by working with patients in acute pain in a project led by Dr. Gert Müller-Schwefe.

At present, Flatischler is collaborating with leading scientists and doctors to investigate the effect of the TaKeTiNa process on the synchronization of the autonomic nervous system. The following methods are being used in this context:

• Measurement of the heart variability rate (HVR). Dr. Lohniger (www.autonomhealth.com) has developed a visual method that shows the development of the HVR online in recognizable images, enabling rapid diagnostics. Dr. Lohninger works together with IBM Zurich and the Vienna Philharmonic, among others. The results of the first two years of research have shown that the TaKeTiNa method results in significant relaxation of the autonomic nervous system as well as a resynchronization of body rhythms. These results can be repeated and replicated.

• Online EEG derivation with Dr. Michael A. Überall show how brain wave patterns develop, change and synchronize during the course of the TaKeTiNa process. Here as well, synchronization processes in the gamma range indicate that highly energetic and connected states of consciousness are induced.

For updated information please visit our website: www.taketina.com Please note: TaKeTiNa is a registered trademark and may only be used by certified TaKeTiNa Teachers.

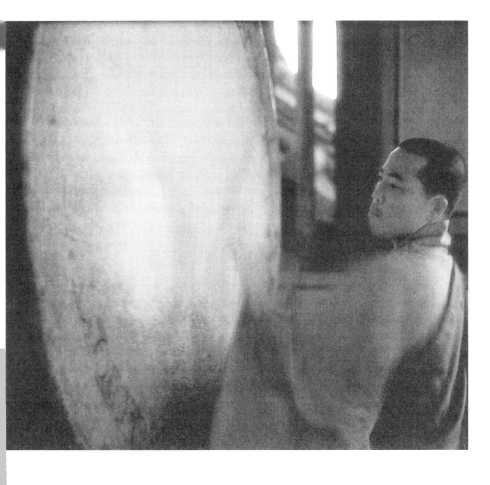

REINHARD FLATISCHLER
DISCOGRAPHY

MEGADRUMS - SCHINORE, 1986
Flatischlers first album that has become legendary. It includes Pandit Arjun Shejwal, one of the greatest master ever on the Indian pakhawaj drum. Pandit Arjun Shejwal died 1992.
Pandit Arjun Shejwal (Pakhawaj), India; Dudu Tucci (Conga), Brazil; Reinhard Flatischler (Tschanggo, Tabla), Austria; Wolfgang Puschnig (Saxophone, Flute), Austria; The Megadrums Percussion Ensemble.

MEGADRUMS - COREANA , 1987
"Rhythm detaches itself form the role of accompaniment and becomes the driving force of the musical composition - an important message for jazz", says the Jazzforum in its presentation of *Coreana*. One of the few productions with the original Samulnori group from Korea.
SamulNori (Tschanggo, Buk, Tsching, Guengari), Korea; Aja Addy (Dondo), Ghana; Dudu Tucci (Conga, brazilian percussion), Brazil; Wolfgang Puschnig (Saxophone, Flute), Austria; Reinhard Flatischler (Tschanggo, Rantang, Buk), Austria; The Megadrums Percussion Ensemble.

MEGADRUMS - TRANSFORMATION , 1990
The last production with Aja Addy - the famous talking drummer from Ghana, who died 2002 in a concert in Korea.
Leonard Eto, (Taiko), Japan; Milton Cardona (Conga, Bata), USA, Aja Addy (Dondo), Ghana; Reinhard Flatischler (Buk, Gongs, Tabla), Austria; Wolfgang Puschnig (Saxophone, Flute), Austria; The Megadrums Percussion Ensemble.

MEGADRUMS - KETU, 1993
For the first time Flatischler combined a complete Gamalan orchestra with jazz-musicians and drummers from around the word. To be able to compose and arrange for this group Flatischler intensively studied all the different instruments in Bali.
Suar Agung (Jegog) Bali, Leonard Eto (Taiko), Zakir Hussain (Tabla), Wolfgang Puschnig (Saxophone, Flute), Reinhard Flatischler (Buk, Tschanggo, Rantang)

MEGADRUMS - LAYERS OF TIME, 1995
..."if ever there is a need to find an universal language of rhythm, this album will be milestone!" (El Pais). A bestselling CD in DolbySurround....
Airto Moreira (Drums, Percussion), Zakir Hussain (Tabla), Glen Velez (Framdrums), Milton Cardona, (Bata, Conga), Valerie Naranjo (mallets, percussion) Wolfgang Puschnig (Saxophone, Flute), Reinhard Flatischler (Bata, Buk, Tschanggo, Rantang)

MEGADRUMS - THE WORLD IS FULL OF RHYTHM, 1999
The World is Full of Rhythm is a compilation of the best musical moments from 15 years of MegaDrums (1984 - 1999). It is one of the most brilliant works in the history of percussion music and certainly Flatischler´s masterwork (www.discover.de)

MEGADRUMS - TERRA NOVA, 2000
There is not only an incredible virtuosity unfolding when these musicians play together, it is also the great compositions and the excellent sound quality which makes this CD so wonderfull to listen to. (Callasong.de)
Airto Moreira (Drums, Percussion), Zakir Hussain (Tabla), Glen Velez (Framdrums), Milton Cardona, (Bata, Conga), Leonard Eto (Taiko), Stephen Kent (Didgeridoo), Cornelia Flatischler (Mallets, Buk), Reinhard Flatischler (Buk, Tschanggo, Mallets, Conga)

LifeRhythm Publications

Anna Halprin   RETURNING TO HEALTH
with Dance, Movement & Imagery
195 pages, illustrations

In this graceful and practical book Anna Halprin offers the wisdom of her life experience as a dancer, teacher and healer. As a cancer survivor, she tells her own story and that of many others with deep compassion and uplifting clarity. Originally written as a manual for teachers, this book is filled with guidance and insights into the emotional processes of a health crisis – as well as clear guidelines for leading groups and lesson plans for classes in healing movement.

Cousto   THE COSMIC OCTAVE
Origin of Harmony
128 pages, 45 illustrations, numerous tables

Cousto demonstrates the direct relationship of astronomical data, such as the frequency of planetary orbits, to ancient and modern measuring systems, the human body, music and medicine. This book is compelling reading for all who wonder if a universal law of harmony does exist behind the apparent chaos of life. Tuning forks, tuned to the planets, earth, sun and moon, according to Cousto's calculations are also available from LifeRhythm.

Helmut G. Sieczka   CHAKRA BREATHING
A Pathway to Energy and Harmony
100 pages, illustrations

A guide to self-healing, this book is meant to help activate and harmonize the energy centers of the subtle body. The breath is the bridge between body and soul. In today's world as our lives are determined by stressful careers and peak performance, the silent and meditative moments have become more vital. Remembering our true selves, our natural energy balances are restored. Chakra-breathing enhances this kind of awareness and transformational work, especially on the emotional and energetic level.

Allan Sachs D.C.   GRAPEFRUIT SEED EXTRACT
A Natural Alternative to Antibiotics
100 pages

Dr. Allan Sachs' innovative work in treating sufferers from Candida Albicans imbalance, fool allergies and environmental illness has inspired thousands of patients and a generation of like-minded physicians. Based on his training as a medical researcher at New York's Downstate Medical Center and his life-long interest in plants, he undertook an intense study of the antimicrobial aspects of certain plant derivatives. This complete handbook gives all information on the theraputic use of grapefruit seeds and also details their use for many household, farming and industrial needs.

Bodo Baginski & Shalila Sharamon   REIKI   Universal Life Energy
200 pages, illustrations

This was the first book ever written about Reiki and it was a runaway best seller. Reiki is described as the energy which forms the basis of all life. With the help of specific methods, anyone can learn to awaken and activate this universal life energy so that healing and harmonizing energy flows through the hands. Reiki is healing energy in the truest sense of the word, leading to greater individual harmony and attunement to the basic forces of the universe. This book features a unique compilation and interpretation, from the author's experience, of over 200 psychosomatic symptoms and diseases.

LIFERHYTHM
Books for Life Changes

Connects you with your Core and entire being – guided by Science, Intuition and Love.

We provide the tools for growth, therapy, holistic health and higher education through publications, seminars and workshops.

If you are interested in our forthcoming projects and want to be on our mailing list, you may let us know by contacting us at:

PO Box 806   Mendocino, CA 95460   USA
www.LifeRhythm.com
email: books@LifeRhythm.com